DO NOT LOSE HOPE

Do Not Lose Hope

Healing the Wounded Heart of Women
Who Have Had Abortions

REV. WILLIAM F. MAESTRI

ALBA·HOUSE   NEW·YORK

SOCIETY OF ST. PAUL, 2187 VICTORY BLVD., STATEN ISLAND, NEW YORK 10314

ST PAULS

Library of Congress Cataloging-in-Publication Data

Maestri, William F.
    Do not lose hope: healing the wounded heart of women who
have had abortions / William F. Maestri.
        p.   cm.
    Includes bibliographical references.
    ISBN 0-8189-0830-0
    1. Abortion — Religious aspects — Christianity.   2. Abortion —
Psychological aspects.   I. Title.
    HQ767.25.M34   2000
    241'.6976 — dc21   99-37223
                                                                        CIP

Nihil Obstat:
Rev. Dennis J. Hayes
Censor Librorum

Imprimatur:
✠ Most Rev. Francis B. Schulte
Archbishop of New Orleans
February 8, 1999

The Nihil Obstat and Imprimatur are official declarations that a book or
pamphlet is free of doctrinal error. No implication is contained therein
that those who have granted the Nihil Obstat and Imprimatur agree with
the contents, opinions or statements expressed.

Produced and designed in the United States of America by the
Fathers and Brothers of the Society of St. Paul,
2187 Victory Boulevard, Staten Island, New York 10314-6603,
as part of their communications apostolate.

ISBN: 0-8189-0830-0

Printing Information:

Current Printing - first digit   1   2   3   4   5   6   7   8   9   10

Year of Current Printing - first year shown

2000   2001   2002   2003   2004   2005   2006   2007   2008

Dedicated to
Mary Ann Glendon
who in every
way helps to build
the civilization
of
Life and Love

Table of Contents

Introduction

"Father, I haven't been to confession and communion in just about twenty years," this woman said to me as she fought back tears.

She is a mother, a wife, and a woman who had an abortion many years ago.

She hasn't missed Mass. She doesn't venture to receive the Eucharist.

She had never made peace with her past and remains tormented in her present. There seems to be no future to hope in.

Until now.

Hope.

Healing.

What occasioned this start of the journey home to the Lord's house and table? To sit in that chair long vacant? Grace to be sure. Grace working through poor, limited secondary sources called human beings.

To be specific, a homily I preached on Pro-Life Sunday directed to women (and adolescents) who have had abortions. This was not novel on my part. I was simply following the example of Pope John Paul II in *Evangelium Vitae* (*The Gospel of Life*). For in his encyclical he addresses a "special word to women who have had an abortion."

I simply proclaimed and amplified on that "special word."

My preaching did *not* immediately bear fruit. This woman

happened (grace always works in such happen-stance) to have children who were preparing for First Reconciliation. I happened to fill in for the pastor who was to present the seminar for parents.

"Father, I was in church with my family and heard your sermon to women who had abortions. I felt you were talking to me. I've been waiting for the chance to see you."

With 1.5 million abortions each year, there are many women who are waiting for healing. They too are victims of abortions.

"I felt like I could never return to Church or the sacraments," she continued. "I knew I did something wrong but I didn't feel like there was a way back."

Yet isn't this just what Jesus as the Way, Truth, and Life is about? The way back.

In our preaching and teaching on life issues, we must be ever mindful of the women who have had abortions. Our truth must have love as its foundation. We must reach out in compassion toward the millions of women who see no way back. We must be ever ready to extend the kiss of peace and oil of gladness. This in no way diminishes the "Respect Life" ministry. Rather, it enhances it by broadening the work of reconciliation. Respect Life takes on a new depth of healing.

The young mother received sacramental reconciliation. She continued her sacramental journey with the Sunday Eucharist. Her story is one that is at once tragic and hopeful. Tragic in that the wound in her heart was left so long unattended. Hopeful in that God's grace never gives up and persists in seeking after us.

The next day I was administering the Sacrament of Reconciliation before the Saturday Vigil Mass. Someone entered the confessional in order to retain her privacy. A woman, whom I judged to be in her mid to late sixties, began in the following manner: "Are you Father Maestri?" she inquired in a hushed and timid tone. "Yes," I said.

"I heard your sermon about women who had abortions," she said as she began to cry.

"I didn't have an abortion but I got an abortion for my daughter," she said fighting to get the words out before the sobs took over. "I was simply afraid of what would be said about my daughter," she continued, "and I just wanted to save her reputation. I know what I did was very wrong."

This woman of upscale means turned to abortion as a way to avoid "the scandal of a pregnant daughter in a Catholic high school." Such avoidance never brings peace.

"I haven't been in a confessional in over thirty-years," she said. "I heard what you preached and I felt this was my chance."

A second chance. So much of Jesus' ministry is directed to those who need second chances (and seven times seventy chances): the tax collectors, publicans, women of ill repute, and an apostle whose three denials became three professions of faith. Women who have had abortions are looking for second chances. Two women separated by the generations yet united through abortion. Such a sisterhood-in-suffering must become a sisterhood-in-healing.

What follows is a series of reflections (not sophisticated moral theology though such is always welcomed) about the defining moral issue of our time — abortion. The focus is on the women of abortion without losing sight of the unborn. The framework for these reflections is Section 99 of John Paul II's encyclical *The Gospel of Life*. The content is provided by those women who have found their voices as they journey from despair to hope, death to life.

As a priest whose ministry has been mainly in the education of women (and being educated *by women*), I have been at once saddened and humbled by the stories of the women of

abortion I have come to know. Saddened because of their loss
and pain. Saddened because so many continue to hurt and
face each day apart from the Church. I am humbled at the
courage so many exhibit who face what happened, claim responsibility and accept John Paul's invitation to be "promoters of a new way of looking at human life."

I am in the debt of Carol Brunies and Lisa Tusa who care-
fully typed and corrected the entire manuscript. I am grateful to the Society of Saint Paul, Alba House, for publishing
these reflections. May they help the pastoral ministry of those
entrusted with the care of souls. May they help women who
have had abortions to not lose hope. Finally, I am most grateful to all the women who have shared their stories. Through
your stripes many will be healed.

William F. Maestri
Notre Dame Seminary
New Orleans, Louisiana

I patiently waited, Lord, for you to hear my prayer.
You listened and pulled me from a lonely pit...
You let me stand on a rock with my feet firm,
and you gave me a new song, a song of praise
to you.
Many will see this and they will honor and
trust you, the Lord God. (Psalm 40:1-3)

The Gospel of Life (No. 99)

I would now like to say a special word
to *women who have had an abortion.*
The Church is aware of the many factors
which may have influenced your decision,
and she does not doubt that in many cases
it was a painful and even shattering decision.
The wound in your heart may not yet have healed.
Certainly what happened was and remains terribly wrong.
But do not give in to discouragement and do not lose hope.
Try rather to understand what happened and face it honestly.
If you have not already done so,
give yourselves over with humility and trust to repentance.
The Father of mercies is ready to give you
his forgiveness and his peace
in the Sacrament of Reconciliation.
You will come to understand that nothing is definitively lost
and you will also be able to ask forgiveness from your child,
who is now living in the Lord.
With the friendly and expert help and advice of other people,
and as a result of your own painful experience,
you can be among the most eloquent defenders
of everyone's right to life.
Through your commitment to life,
whether by accepting the birth of other children
or by welcoming and caring for those
most in need of someone to be close to them,
you will become promoters of a new way of looking at human life.

A Special Word

"When it comes to women's issues the Catholic Church has nothing to say to me."

These angry words from a young adult Catholic woman are all too common. Throwing caution to the wind I decided to press her further. "What is it," I asked, "that makes you so angry when it comes to the Catholic Church?"

"I simply don't think the Church understands women," she said in a somewhat calmer but no less determined manner. "The Church has a whole set of rules especially about sex, but there seems to be a lack of love."

"Can you give me an example?" I asked, hoping to find ground to start a dialogue.

"Sure," she snapped. "The Catholic Church is against abortion. I think abortion is wrong but there is more to it than being against abortion."

"Such as?" I interjected.

"Such as the women who have had abortions. There never seems to be any mention of their needs. I know of a lot of women who are hurting."

"So does the Pope," I offered.

"The Pope?!", she repeated with anger rising again. "This Pope has been very hard on women," she declared in an infallible manner that would have pleased any pontiff.

"Have you read the Pope's encyclical on life issues, especially the sections on abortion?" I asked.

"No," she said, "I don't have any need to read that stuff. The Church and the Pope have their rules. None of it speaks to me or women today."

Again, the following exchange between myself and this student from one of my classes has a familiar sound. Women who are angry, frustrated and hurt are not well informed about the Catholic Church or *this* Pope. This makes it all the more important that the Church's moral teaching *and* pastoral ministry reach women. This is one of our most urgent challenges. And Pope John Paul II is more than up to the task.

Contrary to media distortions, Pope John Paul II has been keenly aware and appreciative of the contributions of women to Church and society. The Holy Father has gone so far as to call for a "new feminism" based on the dignity of women and their unique vocation on behalf of life. For it is women who are often the first teachers of the need to respect life in all its forms. Women teach, in a powerful way, that *each* person is to be respected as an image of God. By this teaching of the need to respect the dignity of each person, women are the most effective agents of building the civilization of life and love.

Women have also suffered in a unique way from the culture of death. Specifically, women have suffered from abortion. And it is to the women of abortion that John Paul II addresses a word that is at once surprising and special.

A Surprising Word

The Pope's word to women is surprising. You may expect to be given a moral lecture on "cleaning up your act." This is especially true when it comes to abortion, which the Pope has defined as the fundamental moral issue of our time. You may expect to be scolded and made to feel even more guilty. Yet in place of a finger-wagging Pope, we encounter a Pastor who is reaching out to women who are hurting and in need of healing. There is teaching with love; moral truth proclaimed with the compassion of God's grace.

A Special Word

The Pope's word is also special. Within the flow of the encyclical, *The Gospel of Life,* there comes a word which serves as a speed-bump. In other words, slow down and don't put the Pope's message on cruise control. You are about to encounter something out of the ordinary. The Pope is not preaching to the choir. He wants to talk to the heart of women who have had abortions. And his words are truth, love, and life. In his few, simple words there is a profound attempt to reach out to women who are hurting and in need of healing. The truth the Pope speaks is offered with love.

Women of Abortion

Who are the women of abortion? Who are the women for whom the Pope offers his surprising and special words? With 1.2 to 1.5 million abortions yearly in America alone, the women of abortion are our daughters, wives, relatives, friends, and members of our parish. We work with women who have had abortions. We teach them in our classes. We pass them on the street. Too often they are carrying a secret wound that is reopened by the sound of a child or the sight of an expectant mother.

The Pope is not concerned with statistics but with the story of each woman. It is a story that is not complete. It is a story in search of an ending, a healing. That will come fully only in eternity. For now the journey home must begin with this special word from John Paul II. A great courage will be required to tell one's story. The willingness to acknowledge loss, accept responsibility, enter grieving, and move toward reconciliation calls for an openness to grace. All of this is a hard mercy to be sure. But there is no other way. Unfortunately our culture counsels privacy and a false comfort through freedom of choice. The Pope's special word counsels the need for solidarity and the healing which comes through that authentic freedom guided by truth.

Woman at the Well

The Gospel of John contains a number of stories about individuals who meet Jesus. One of the most powerful is the encounter between Jesus and the Samaritan woman (Jn 4:4-41).

She is a woman with a past. This unnamed Samaritan woman has been married five times and the man she is living with is not her husband. We might expect Jesus to give her a stern moral lecture. Not so. No doubt she has had many such lectures to no avail. This woman needs the words of Jesus. For his words are spirit and life.

After speaking with Jesus this woman with a past is now a woman with a future. In spite of her past, or maybe *because* of her past, she is able to carry the message about Jesus to her fellow Samaritans.

This woman tells her townsfolk: "He told me everything I have done" (Jn 4:39). Imagine, Jesus knew all about her past, yet it did not cause him to turn her away. On the contrary, this woman became a messenger for the One who brings living waters. Wonder of wonder, on the basis of her word, "the Samaritans came to him, they invited him to stay with them; and he stayed there two days" (Jn 4:40). Her testimony makes possible hospitality; new life between enemies — Jews and Samaritans. In fact, after Jesus moves on, others in the town come to believe, to know "that this is truly the savior of the world" (Jn 4:42).

Women at the Well — Today

The story of the Samaritan woman at the well is not frozen in the Bible but occurs each time we encounter Jesus, each time we look for that life-giving water which offers a new beginning. Today there is a special need for such waters by women who have had abortions. Yes, there is a past which causes hurt and shame. Yes, there are those who condemn and reject sinners as well as the sins.

But there is also the possibility of rebirth. There is the possibility of carrying the Gospel of life to other women hurt by abortion. There is the hope that one's past sin can become an opportunity to teach about life and to help other women suffering the effects of an abortion. Often women who have had abortions do not trust. Fear closes one's heart. Shame prevents one from sharing her story. There is a silence which confines the hurt and prevents healing. It is often through women who have had abortions, and have been healed, that so much ministry to others in a similar situation can be accomplished. They can make others feel free to share their stories without condemnation or the need to over explain. There is a recognition which comes from having been bonded through the tragedy of abortion. There can also be that union in spirit which comes from encountering Jesus and being healed.

The disciples see Jesus talking to a woman (a Samaritan at that!) and are amazed. In that gesture, all of the cultural, social, and religious barriers which had served to divide and isolate were overcome. To Jesus the future is more important than the past; the new possibility is more exciting than the old failure; out of sin can come the greater abundance of grace.

The disciples in their amazement do not ask the question which was on all their minds, "What are you looking for?" or, "Why are you talking with her?" Such a silence is *not* golden. We must ask of Jesus, "What are you looking for?" The response of Jesus is clear, "Disciples who will be reborn in my life-giving waters and bring these waters to refresh others." We must ask of Jesus, "Why are you talking with her?" The answer of Jesus is simple, "Because she is just such a disciple."

Pope John Paul II addresses a special word to women who have had abortions. No doubt this will amaze many. There are those who believe that such women deserve no special word except a word of condemnation. This is not the way of Jesus. There are those who believe that any word from the Pope is a noisy gong and clanging cymbal. The Pope and the Catholic Church have nothing to say to women. This is not the way of John Paul. For, from the center of his heart as shepherd, he speaks to the heart of women who have had abortions. In imitation of the Good Shepherd, this Pope proclaims a message of forgiveness and healing.

Listen to his voice and find repose in verdant pastures besides those restful waters which can refresh your soul (Ps 23; Jn 10:1-18).

A Painful and Shattering Experience

J ENNY IS A BRIGHT 20 YEAR-OLD college student at a
prestigious university. She is a good student and popular
with peers and faculty. Jenny did not go steady in high
school but enjoyed the company of various young men.
She came to college free of a high school sweetheart and
was determined to remain so. However, the heart has its
power which the will underestimates and the mind
cannot fathom. Jenny became intensely involved with a
graduate student. Predictably, the romance ended as
abruptly as it began. The fact that Jenny became
pregnant helped cool the passion. She found herself
alone, away from home, and facing a profound decision.
Jenny was assured by the culture and personal friends
that abortion was "the solution to her problem." The
abortion provider promised a quick fix to "her situation
so she could move on." Painfully Jenny came to realize
that abortion is anything but a solution. Her situation
was only made worse by the choice of abortion.

The Many Factors

Abortion is not simply about choice. Abortion is not just
a simple exercise of an option or a consumer preference.
Abortion is about life and death. The effects of the decision
to abort linger long after the deed. Abortion is not, contrary

to the propaganda of the abortion industry, a simple exercise of a "fundamental right." There are many factors which enter into the abortion decision.

The litany of reasons for abortion is a familiar one: the fear of interrupting a career or education; fear of social condemnation because of pregnancy outside of marriage; fear of disappointing one's parents or significant others; fear of being abandoned by the child's father; and fear of having to raise a child alone. So much that surrounds the abortion decision is motivated by fear. Fear does not lessen the objective wrongness of abortion but it can diminish the moral guilt attributed to the woman. The First Letter of John teaches that fear is overcome by love. We read: "There is no fear in love; but perfect love casts out fear. For fear has to do with punishment, and the one who fears is not made perfect in love" (1 Jn 4:18).

The aftermath of abortion continues to imprison one in fear. There is the fear of being exposed to the judgment of family and friends. There is the fear of being rejected forever by God. There is the fear that the abortion decision will cause God's wrath to be visited on one's future children. For example, when I was a young priest a woman presented herself at the rectory door greatly upset and seeking prayers.

"Could you pray for my little boy who is going to get operated on tomorrow?" asked this woman who was doing her best not to cry. "Of course I will," I said. "Is it a serious operation?" I inquired.

"It's for a hernia," she said, "and the doctors keep telling me there's nothing to worry about. But I...."

Her voice faded into a silence which clearly indicated that more than medical reassurance was needed.

I sensed there was something more than the request of an overly concerned mother for her child.

"Is there something else that is bothering you?" I asked.

"Even with the assurances of the doctors you seem very concerned."

"It's just that I don't want anything to happen to my boy," she said as she kept looking at her fingers and avoiding any eye contact.

"What are you afraid might happen?" I pressed her.

"Maybe God won't hear my prayers," she said in a way that indicated she wanted me to contradict her concern.

"Why do you think God won't hear your prayers?" I asked.

"If you do something real bad," she said now looking at me, "will God punish those you love?"

"God doesn't deal with us that way," I tried to assure her. "God wants to forgive us. Jesus came to forgive our sins. God certainly wouldn't hurt an innocent person because of the sins of another."

She paused a few moments and responded, "What if that person did something real bad?"

"It doesn't matter," I said, "the greater our sin the more we need God's grace. Again, God doesn't try to get back at us. Even less would God hurt somebody we love."

I sensed this woman needed some encouragement in speaking about her past. There was more here than a distraught mother looking for divine help. This was a woman in need of release from her past.

"Would it help to talk about what's hurting you?" I asked.

"I'm not sure I can find the words," she said softly. "I've never talked about this."

I suggested that before we talked we pray together.

After some minutes in prayer she opened her heart to grace and found her voice: "When I was young... I... I had an abortion," and almost as if to make sure she got it all out, "I am so sorry and I don't want God to take my little boy."

We spent quite some time in talking about God, *her* story

of God, her past relationships, and more importantly her *present* need.

She seemed relieved at last to share the burden and to be assured of God's love. She agreed to see the pastor so she could be reconciled to the Church and receive the Eucharist. Finally, she said she would call me tomorrow after her son's surgery.

She kept that promise. The little boy did fine. Every now and then I would see her at Mass. She seemed so different from that woman who showed up at the rectory door. Over the years we have lost contact, but I often think of her and of how many other women have similar stories.

This woman was in the grip of fear; fear of what she had done and fear of what she believed God was about to do. It was only God's love which was able to break the grip of fear. God's love empowers us to face the truth, accept the past, express contrition, and acknowledge our healing. Women of abortion are especially in need of that love which drives out all fear. Women who decide to abort their children are overwhelmed with feelings of shame, guilt, self-loathing, and a profound unworthiness which can lead to despair. A desperation sets in, and women begin to feel there is no road back. This is why it is so important to assure such women that God is Love. They must come to know that heaven celebrates their reconciliation. There is a joy, long denied them, which makes new life possible.

Pain and Suffering

Jenny, our 20 year-old coed, was assured by her abortion provider that the whole procedure was painless.

"The impression I got," said Jenny, "was that an abortion

was no different than a tooth extraction or having my tonsils removed." In the beginning this was the case. She put a great deal of energy in denial and emotionally numbing herself for what was about to happen. Yet the denial and numbing do not last. The reality of abortion breaks through the defense mechanisms.

It is not uncommon for women to sign the consent forms with tears. There is a deep sadness, an initial feeling of loss and bereavement, that cannot be repressed. The rhetoric of "rights" and "free choice" are of little consolation. The woman knows that there is more to the life living within her than a mere collection of cells, a blob of tissue, or a pre-embryo. Living within her is a unique human being waiting to be born. Living within is *her* child.

It is not uncommon for women to experience a good deal of pain after an abortion. The body refuses to join in the charade that abortion is no big deal; a little rest and "you'll be as good as new." There can be bleeding as well as intense abdominal pain following an abortion. There can also be hormonal changes that cause severe emotional swings. The woman knows that her abortion is a big deal and it will take more than a few days to be as good as new.

The post-traumatic condition of women who have had abortions is not only physical pain. There is psychological and spiritual suffering which women experience. The date of the abortion and the date when the child would have been born cause a deep anguish. These reminders, along with flashbacks of the abortion triggered by the sound of a child or an expectant mother, can send women into a deep depression. Jenny remembers one incident in particular. While heading to an afternoon class she saw the secretary of one of her professors. For the first time Jenny noticed the woman was pregnant. Jenny began to well up with tears and could not attend her class.

"I felt so stupid and embarrassed," she recalls, "but above all I was filled with such a deep sense of remorse."

There is also the spiritual suffering which women experience.

"For the longest time I wouldn't even pass a church," said Jenny.

"It was a reminder of what I did. The feelings of guilt would just overwhelm me."

Jenny's avoidance of Church is not uncommon. At some level women know that they are in need of a healing which goes deeper than the physical and psychological. There is the need for spiritual healing. Yet the very source of that healing is too often viewed as a source of condemnation and punishment. It is crucial that women come to experience the Church as a community of life, love, and forgiveness.

The Church

The challenge for the Church to reach out in compassion to the women of abortion is clearly voiced by John Paul II. In talking about the pain and suffering women experience, the Pope indicates that "the Church is aware" of both the complexity and the anguish surrounding abortion. In effect, the Pope is placing the Church in solidarity with the women of abortion. These women are not alone. They are not to be abandoned. They are to hear and experience the Gospel of Life. While the culture views abortion as trivial, and hence the pain of women as well, the Church takes with utmost seriousness the *total* experience of women who have had abortions. The Church does not offer cheap grace and a quick absolution. Rather, the Church listens to the story of each woman. These stories are complex, painful, and in need of healing.

The Church ministers to women in such a way that acceptance of responsibility does not culminate in despair. On the contrary, the acceptance of responsibility is a crucial step on the path to healing.

The experience of abortion leaves women with a deep wound. The mere passage of time does not bring healing. The depth of this wound is often ignored by our society and even by those in the psychiatric community. This wound has not escaped John Paul. It is to the unhealed wound in the heart of the women of abortion that we now turn.

Wound in Your Heart

D EBORAH IS A 40 YEAR-OLD African-American who grew up in
southern California and now resides in the South.
She is a college graduate, employed by a well known
restaurant in an executive management position. To her
most intimate friends and mere acquaintances, Deborah
has it all together: successful career, the respect of
colleagues, and a seat in first class on the fast track of
upper level management, if not out and out ownership
of her own business. There is nothing but blue skies and
green lights for Deborah. Yet there is a sadness that
lies just below the surface. Deborah expends a great deal
of energy keeping the sadness hidden. However, there
are moments when waves of guilt, shame, self-loathing,
and anger wash away the most cheery of exteriors. It was
not supposed to be this way. Deborah was told that
abortion is quickly obtained and easily forgotten.
Deborah was told she should feel grateful that our
society allows abortion. Deborah was not told the truth.
There is still a wound in her heart. There are nights
when Deborah cannot sleep, or if she does, she is
awakened by disturbing nightmares. Pills are becoming
more frequent along with alcohol consumption. As a
teenager Deborah had an abortion, pressured by an
older man who promised "to walk" if she didn't "do what
was right by both of us." She had the abortion.
Predictably, he left anyway. Deborah is at the point
where she can no longer take the pain. Pills, the bottle,

and being in and out of therapy no longer provide relief. More and more she wonders "if it's all worth it."

Abortion is presented as painless as well as victimless. The unborn child is viewed as simply a glob of tissue. The woman is merely exercising a fundamental right to a "medical procedure." The recovery time for women is no more than that for a tooth extraction or a tonsillectomy. In no time she will be resuming life as usual. The abortion industry invests an enormous amount of energy in assuring women that nothing significant has happened. In fact, the abortion industry does its best to make women grateful for this "solution to their problem."

In time women come to see the fallacy and folly of trivializing abortion. Contrary to the propaganda, the women of abortion experience the following: flashbacks of the abortion procedure; drug and alcohol abuse; eating disorders; unstable relationships; frantic attempts to keep busy through work or volunteer activities; unexpected waves of sadness and crying along with feelings of guilt, shame, and self-loathing which cause great pain. Unfortunately, the woman must face all of these experiences alone. Panic usually sets in and the woman begins to act in a trivial and reckless manner. There may also be periods of promiscuous behavior. Such episodes only add to the guilt and shame.

For Deborah the wound left by abortion centers on her self-image. Deborah prides herself on being in control. She is the one others come to for guidance. She is the strong and wise one who is able to shoulder whatever life has to offer. However this self-image has been severely challenged by abortion and the post-abortion trauma she experiences. More and more she comes to see herself as vulnerable, out of control, and in danger of losing all she has worked to achieve. Deborah is extremely angry because she feels she was abandoned during her abortion, and she continues to face alone this wound that won't heal. Deborah often finds herself wondering, "So many years have passed and yet there is no relief. Why am I still struggling to get myself together?"

A Grief Denied

The abortion industry and the culture at large advertise abortion as the quick, easy solution to the "problem of an unwanted, unplanned pregnancy." By defining abortion as a "solution" to an unpleasant situation, the message for women is clear: women of abortion, you should be relieved and grateful for "services" provided. If abortion is a service which "fixes" a woman's "situation," then any talk about grief, mourning, and loss is strangely out of place. There is no room for guilt or shame. What is appropriate is celebration. However, women who have had abortions find no reason for joy and the "solution" only adds to their burden.

The loss of a child is acutely painful to a mother. The prenatal loss carries a special grief. The birth of a child contains so much hope. Yet such a hope will not be realized. Miscarriage, stillbirth, Sudden Infant Death Syndrome, and ectopic pregnancy are causes for a grieving with an intensity similar to that associated with the loss of an older child. Yet, too often, those who suffer a prenatal loss do not receive the support (from society and Church) they need. Prenatal loss and the subsequent grief can be given too little attention. Parents are left to mourn alone which only increases the pain. However, more and more medical personnel and clergy are being trained in dealing with those who suffer such a loss. Parents are encouraged to hold the child, provide a name, take pictures, celebrate a religious service, and bury the baby with other loved ones. All of this helps parents to work through their grief and form memories which can promote healing.

Psychiatrist M.J. Horowitz presents grief in four stages. The first stage is one of *Outcry*. The parent expresses to others, in hope of consolation, an intense emotional pain. Stage two is the *Denial Phase* in which there is an avoidance of any reminder of the deceased and a kind of emotional numbness which gives some relief from pain. Thirdly, there is the *Intrusion Phase* in which bad memories of the deceased or some unpleasant experiences come to mind. The grieving person finds it difficult to concentrate and perform everyday tasks. Finally, there is *Working Through* in which the bereaved person is able to experience good and bad memories of the deceased. Gone is the denial and the inability to concentrate. Also the bereaved person begins to form new relationships as well as to become involved with work and the demands of life as a whole.

E. Joanne Angelo, also a psychiatrist, draws on the work of Horowitz in discussing the *pathological* manifestations of the grief process. The four stages discussed by Horowitz remain but they "are intensified, prolonged or delayed in their expression, and the bereaved person is not able to resume normal functioning because of the development of other psychiatric or psycho-physiologic symptoms" ("The Negative Impact of Abortion On Women and Families," p. 48).

Here are a few of the pathological manifestations of grief in each stage. With the *Outcry Phase* the person experiences a panic state in which behavior is unpredictable. There are intense bouts of grief and fear along with a general withdrawal from life. In the *Denial Phase* there is a turning to drugs and alcohol for relief. The person may also begin to take risks and seek thrills as a way of affirming life. This attempt to be numb soon passes into the *Intrusion Phase* in which troubling images (nightmares and flashbacks) interfere with work, sleep, and the general business of everyday life. The person becomes increasingly depressed (associated with unresolved grief) and thoughts of suicide become more appealing as the person falls deeper into feelings of unworthiness, guilt, and shame.

Abortion: The Grief That Does Not Speak

The special grief experienced by those who suffer a prenatal loss is magnified for women who have an abortion. The reasons are many: our abortion culture does not validate a woman's grief because of an abortion. On the contrary, she should be relieved that her "problem" has found a "solution." To grieve is to be ungrateful.

The abortion provider (staff as well as physician) does not offer grief counseling or support women in their loss. After all, the obtaining of an abortion is a fundamental right which the woman is exercising as a free citizen. There is no need to help her work through grief.

The woman who has an abortion often does so in silence and secrecy. Her family, significant others, and clergy seldom find out about the abortion. This means she must shoulder the grief alone. The woman is often surprised and angry that after so much time has passed she still experiences the pain of loss as well as waves of guilt and shame. The woman feels a tremendous need to unburden herself, but to whom? Rather than risk rejection and condemnation, the woman suffers in a lonely silence which only increases her pain.

In the case of women who suffer a prenatal loss there is at least the comfort of forming some positive memories. There is often the chance to hold the baby, take pictures, name the child, and provide a proper religious celebration with burial. All of these join together in helping the grieving parents to start their journey of healing. Women of abortion are denied many if not all of these human comforts. If this silent grief continues unattended rather than go away, various dysfunctions become manifest: alcohol and drug abuse, emotional instability, dramatic fluctuations in weight, inability to work and concentrate, waves of guilt and shame, abdominal pain, sexual acting out, increase in family strife marked by the need to intensely control, disturbing dreams about one's aborted baby, sleep disorder, and an intense depression which increases the woman's thoughts of suicide.

The abortion debate may grab the headlines and fill the evening news, but to the women of abortion the *reality* too often remains cloaked in silence. The culture as well as the abortion industry trivializes abortion and with it the plight of women and their grief. The medical and psychiatric communities are often poorly trained in associating abortion with grief and, as a result, are unable to provide effective counseling. For many in the helping professions the clinical signs that the women of abortion evidence are dismissed as usually associated with some other disorder. Women are very reluctant to discuss their abortion with family and friends. The only thing worse than being trivialized is being judged and condemned by loved ones.

To whom can the women of abortion turn?

The Church As Comforter

The image often presented of the Catholic Church when it comes to abortion is not that of comforter but condemner. Rather than a community with arms outstretched, the Church is more an institution with arms folded in a cold, stern manner. The Church does not extend the hand of peace but more often wags its finger at those under the burden of guilt.

Honesty requires us to admit that at times there has been an absence of love in our defense of life. We can too easily forget the frailty of human clay. We can too sternly preach our message of moral truth devoid of compassion. In no way should there be a denial of the terrible wrong that is abortion. But equally important is the need to know that this terrible wrong is never made right by the continuing pain of the mother. In the profound words of Saint Ambrose, "No one is ever healed by hurting another."

The elaborate sacramental system of the Catholic Church, along with its teaching about the Communion of Saints, uniquely positions the Church to provide spiritual healing to the women of abortion. This won't be easy. Women must overcome their fear and the belief that the Church is only interested in condemnation. Yet such healing is possible through the ministry of a pastorally sensitive clergy and women themselves being open to grace. Through the Sacrament of Reconciliation (in a subsequent chapter more about this Sacrament and abortion will be discussed) the Church extends spiritual healing and offers newness of life. The Communion of Saints assures the woman that nothing is permanently lost. Even after death there is a connection between the living and the dead, earth and that life on the other side of the grave. The aborted child is now at peace in the Lord.

That child can pray for the healing of its mother. The mother can be encouraged to talk to the child, acknowledge responsibility, and ask forgiveness. There can even be a memorial service for the aborted child so that there may be some closure afforded the mother.

A Return To Deborah

Deborah is in a dangerous place. She is successful in terms of her career but that is beginning to slip away. She has tried various therapies along with increasing amounts of pills and alcohol. These have offered little relief. In fact, they have only added to her pain. Deborah's struggle has intensified and so has her desire to find some comfort. Long ago the fire of a religious faith was set by her parents.

Unfortunately the years have turned the flame to cold ashes. Recently Deborah has been giving religion a second look. Amid the aches a spark may yet remain. If only that gentle wind of the Spirit would fan that smoldering ember, the flame of faith may yet burn bright. This is an enormous risk for Deborah. She risks facing her past. She must risk responsibility. She must risk hearing the truth in order to be free. In other words, Deborah must find the courage to accept her healing.

It is to this courage to accept healing that we now turn.

Do Not Lose Hope

ESS IS A CATHOLIC IN HER EARLY THIRTIES. She is married and has one child. In recent years she has played the role of full time mom. Much to her surprise she has not missed working. Tess has found a good deal of personal satisfaction in watching her son grow. Before she was married, Tess became pregnant and made the decision to have an abortion. "I knew it was the wrong thing to do almost immediately," she said. "But I felt all kinds of pressure from my boy friend as well as the pressure of trying to finish college."

Tess received a great deal of support for having an abortion. Friends who knew, as well as the staff of the abortion clinic, assured Tess she was doing "the only reasonable thing." The various personnel at the abortion clinic did their best to make Tess believe that she would "soon be back to normal."

Yet things were far from normal. The assurance and rationalizations only increased her inner turmoil. It seemed no one took her situation with the moral seriousness it deserved. Tess did not want an easy way out or a quick absolution. There was more to what took place than the removal of some cells or tissue. Tess always knew she made the decision to end the life of her unborn child. What she wanted was someone to walk with her through the guilt and shame in order to began a true healing. This would only come about by facing abortion in all its terrible violence. Tess found the words of John Paul II at

once realistic, challenging, and hopeful. Here was a
Pope who understood what she was feeling and what she
needed.

We are living in the *Age of Whatever*. I have come to notice more and more the use (and abuse) of the word "whatever" cropping up in daily discourse. From the television to
the classroom, from sit-com stars to students, the word "whatever" enjoys high usage.

I have also come to notice that the one who uses (and
abuses) "whatever" is usually trying to avoid some personal
embarrassment, correction, or a point of unpleasantness.
Rather than accept the correction or engage in a reasonable
discussion, the person simply says, "whatever!" as a way of ending conversation. Each person is left with her initial belief or
position. In other words, the Age of Whatever reduces all
morals and truth to one's private perspective, opinion, or
point of view. There are no objective standards of truth, no
principles that govern reasoned debate, and no universal
moral virtues that direct behavior toward a good end. The Age
of Whatever reduces all of reality to a radical individualism
and subjectivism which accepts feelings as the moral compass
for conduct.

Abortion and The Age of Whatever

The Age of Whatever, with its trivialization of truth and
morality, fits well with abortion. For abortion is never recognized for what it is and never acknowledged for the destruc-
tion it brings. Unfortunately, those in the abortion industry
and well meaning individuals often join forces in "protecting"
the woman who has had an abortion. Such protection is usually wrapped in the blanket of compassion or "a woman's right

to choose." The woman is protected from her deadly choice by an industry which presents the unborn as a mere collection of cells or fetal tissue. She is assured through the misuse of biology that a human life was not lost. Emotional support, in the name of compassion, is given so that the woman can "get on with her life." From the perspective of the abortion industry, in addition to well meaning friends, the message is the same: abortion is no big thing. It is either a solution to an unwanted pregnancy or a private choice that no one can understand. The guilt and shame experienced by women do not find an empathetic ear. Both the abortion industry and friends want to rush to closure so the whole thing can be put behind the woman.

The Age of Whatever is committed to closure of any unpleasantry. There is, however, a danger in closing an open wound too quickly. The body provides a natural washing of open wounds — bleeding. Only after the jagged pieces and dirt are removed can the wound be closed safely. If debris and dirt remain, in a short time there will be fever and infection. The wound will only have to be reopened causing even greater pain. A short term closure is no solution for the long term process of healing. There is simply a pain in body and spirit which must be endured if we are to mature.

The Age of Whatever rushes to close the wound of abortion. It does not allow women the opportunity to grieve or mourn their loss. When women give voice to their anguish about their abortions, the Age of Whatever dismisses their cries as trivial, misguided, and just "a phase." In short order all will be forgotten as one picks up the threads of career, relationships, or education. If women insist on giving voice to their grief, too often they are met with a look of bewilderment, a dismissive wave of the hand, a roll of the eyes, and a frustrated chorus of "whatever."

John Paul: He Understands

"I just couldn't find anyone to listen," said Shannon, "I mean anyone who would listen to *me* and not just my words." Shannon's frustration is not uncommon. Women of abortion desperately seek someone who can understand their pain and the guilt they feel because of their decision. It is so difficult to find such a person when abortion is viewed as a choice, a right, or a medical procedure. It is difficult to express loss, guilt, and shame in a culture which does not view abortion as a great evil. Women need to find a partner in conversation who understands the moral enormity of their decision. Essential to true healing is the need to face honestly the moral gravity of abortion. Only with such honest conversations can women feel they are taken seriously. And it is in these honest, serious conversations that women feel understood.

The Age of Whatever along with its offspring, the culture of death, do their best to convince women that any talk of sin, evil, guilt, shame, and loss is a sign of *their* being victimized by religion. Any turn to a religious faith is viewed as tragic and only dragging women deeper into depression. Women are often told that religion is only about condemnation and judgment. The turn to one's faith produces anything but compassion and healing. The culture of death presents religion as anything but an agent to relieve pain. Rather, religion is presented as a scouring pad which continues to reopen past wounds that should be forgotten.

In spite of this assault by the culture of death on women turning to a religious faith, women can and do break the chains of this ideology. In fact, when women turn to their religious faith they can experience for the first time a deep feeling of being understood. Far from being condemned and rejected, women find that moral truth which begins to liberate them. They are helped to find the language for naming what they did, expressing their feelings of guilt and shame, experiencing contrition, and reaping the fruit of reconciliation.

To the surprise of many, Pope John Paul II has set the moral and pastoral tone for the Catholic Church's ministry to the women of abortion. The Pope's teaching comes as no surprise to those who are even faintly familiar with his life. Here is a Pope who had a life *before* he became John Paul II. Karol Wojtyla was a young man in love with life and people, an individual blessed with intellectual, literary, and artistic gifts which gave him a profound understanding of the human person. Added to his personal gifts was the tragic suffering of his native Poland at the hands of the Nazis and Communists during World War II. All of these influences came together to form a character at once human and deeply spiritual. He is recognized as a man of moral courage yet compassionate toward those who suffer; a priest with a strong faith all the while understanding of those who stumble; a Pope who preaches against the culture of death by advancing the civilization of life and love. It is this man, priest, and Pope who truly understands women who have had abortions.

John Paul II speaks to them the words of moral seriousness and the words of hope: "Certainly what happened was and remains terribly wrong." At last here is a man who understands. Yes, understands that abortion is a terrible wrong. Abortion involves the decision by the mother to end the life of her unborn child. Abortion is an unjust attack on innocent human life. These words of the Pope wake women from their moral slumber often induced by psychiatrists who dispense pills and a culture which offers a drink. John Paul II is saying what women feel while, at the same time, giving them permission to voice their guilt and shame. The silent, secret pain so long hidden can be given voice and brought into the healing light of truth. The Pope does not trivialize abortion and the pain women feel. Just the opposite. Abortion is a terrible wrong and the pain women feel attests to that reality.

The moral seriousness of abortion is joined with words of hope: "But do not give in to discouragement and do not lose hope." Can these words follow from what just went before? Can the Pope who called abortion a terrible wrong be the same Pope who now counsels hope? Is not such talk proof that the Pope wants it both ways — moral sternness while appearing to be compassionate?

John Paul II *does* want it both ways: a serious recognition of the wrongness of abortion *and* the reaching out with hope to women who are tempted to despair. In fact if women are to experience healing there must be this "both-and" approach; both moral truth *and* love; acknowledgment of wrongness *and* hope to begin anew. John Paul knows that if moral truth is separated from hope there can be no true healing. For if all we do is preach a moral truth without hope the result is despair. If all we do is offer hope without an acknowledgment of past wrongs, we trivialize our dignity as morally responsible beings. What the Age of Whatever and the culture of death separate — moral responsibility and hope — John Paul II has joined together for the healing of the women of abortion.

Jesus And Women

Jesus' relationship with women was anything but ordinary. He enjoyed the company of women and he treated them with respect. Jesus was receptive to their hospitality (see the story of Martha and Mary in Luke's Gospel, 10:38-42) and found them stimulating in conversation (check out his conversation with the Samaritan woman at the well in John's Gospel, 4:4-42). Jesus displayed a special sensitivity to women who were burdened by their past. He was able to see in them new possibilities for growth and service. Jesus did not let the past bury the future. Rather, by speaking to women the truth with love, he was able to open up a future they could hope in (Lk 7:36-50; Jn 20:11-18).

In chapter 8 of John's Gospel we read the episode about Jesus and the woman caught in adultery (8:1-11). For our purposes the following is significant: Jesus does not excuse or condone her behavior. She was caught in adultery. Nothing changes the wrongness of her behavior. Jesus respects her too much to excuse her conduct under the guise of abuse: that she was the victim of her husband; a male dominated culture; or a stern religious background. None of these is the issue here. This woman is primary with Jesus; not as some test case but as a human being who can be better than her past.

Jesus is finally alone with this unnamed woman. Gone are her accusers and with them condemnation. Alone in the presence of Jesus there is no condemnation. Both she and Jesus know that what she did was wrong. To acknowledge her actions as sinful is not to reject her as a person. Just the opposite. This woman has committed adultery but there is more to her than adultery. She remains loved by God. In the absence of condemnation she can hear Jesus' words of challenge and hope: "Go and from now on do not sin any more." Jesus ministers to this woman with a mixture of moral truth and hope in order to produce a balm that heals.

It is just such a medicine that the women of abortion need. Our culture does not pick up stones to throw, but offers an array of excuses to trivialize sin. Churches must be ever vigilant that, in defending life, they do not forget to offer hope and healing. Too often women have been made "to stand in the middle" of those who carry the stones of condemnation. This is not the way of Jesus; not the way of John Paul II; and it cannot be the way of the Catholic Church.

Jesus' encounter with the woman caught in adultery reveals the God we dare call our Father. Not a cold, aloof God who is indifferent to our joys and sorrows. Rather, Jesus reveals the living God who is the Father of mercies. Such a mercy is not sentimental but one that allows for true repentance. The mercy that Jesus extends comes from the Father who understands.

The Father of Mercies

ULIE IS A CATHOLIC IN HER MID TO late forties. She would object to such a characterization. What is objectionable is not her age but being identified as a Catholic. "I was baptized a Catholic," said Julie with no attempt to hide her anger, "but it doesn't count since I wasn't asked. It doesn't mean a thing to me now." (Julie is strangely angry over something that "doesn't mean a thing to me now.") Just out of high school, Julie had a summer romance which ended with her being pregnant. She was ready to begin her college studies and a child just didn't fit in. Also her parents would have "flipped out." She never told the boy involved. Her pregnancy was a secret and her abortion as well. Whenever the issue of abortion came up in conversation with friends, the "e" word would always come up — EXCOMMUNICATION. She had been told that abortion and excommunication go hand and hand. "It just figured to be right," said Julie with obvious disgust, "the Church just wants to put people out. You'd think it would be just the opposite. But no way."

Julie has never married though she did experience some long-term relationships. "Nothing serious," said Julie with a wave of the hand, "I don't know if I'll ever be ready for that kind of commitment."

Julie has had no formal, sustained contact with the Church for many years. "There was a priest I used to talk to," confided Julie, "but he got moved to another state.

Figures...." There is a sadness in Julie's voice which gives one the impression that this priest would have been a bridge for reconnecting with the Church. Perhaps she will meet another such priest.

Understanding and Honesty

John Paul II does not only offer women understanding. He also challenges the women of abortion "to understand what happened and face it honestly." Understanding and honesty go together so that hope can replace discouragement.

Understanding is a gift of the Holy Spirit and differs from a mere awareness of facts. More is required than reporting data in some kind of scientific, objective fashion. Such cold precision merely swims on the surface and does not plunge the depth of human experience *and* God's grace. Abortion is not a simple choice, a removal of tissue or cells, the exercise of a reproductive right, or an expression of liberation. Abortion is the decision to end the life of one's child. And that child is innocent. The guilt, shame, and loss that one feels are signs of the gravity of that decision. Hence, such feelings indicate that abortion is no trivial matter. Such feelings break through one's defense mechanisms, denials, and a cultural ideology which devalues life in the womb. Far from being signs of pathology, these feelings are an indication that one is in need of repentance and healing. To understand what is going on inside (biologically and spiritually) requires courage.

The courage for such an understanding means we look at the decision to abort with honesty. This is never easy. Excuses abound but are not accepted. Abortion is honestly understood as an unjust attack on innocent human life. Such honesty is viewed as harsh and judgmental by our "moral Jell-O" culture. In the name of "compassion" we are told to be understanding. However, that kind of understanding runs close to condoning what was done or trivializing the woman's decision. Authentic honesty does not condone, trivialize, offer cheap compassion, or pretend nothing significant occurred. Authentic honesty is one with reality. That is, honesty takes account of the "many factors which may have influenced" the decision. Honesty accepts responsibility for the decision. It is this honesty when joined with a Spirit-filled understanding that moves one closer to repentance and healing.

Humility and Trust

Humility is not self-hatred. Pope John Paul II is calling the women of abortion to face the truth of what they did, accept responsibility, and grow into repentance. Such a process is really a journey in proper self-love and respect. Self-hatred comes from the denial of what was done, the refusal to accept responsibility, and the turning of guilt feelings destructively inward. There is no repentance and no healing.

Humility is not humiliation. Pope John Paul II is acknowledging the dignity of the woman who has had an abortion by recognizing her freedom and responsibility. The call to repentance is the recognition that one can change and overcome the past. Repentance is not self-hatred and self-pity but a firm resolution to reform and live a new way.

No doubt there is a nagging doubt; a subliminal message that cautions — "Don't be a fool. You can't trust anything the Church teaches. You are nothing but a sinner in the hands of an angry God." This message is strong and receives powerful play in our anti-religious culture. Honesty demands that we acknowledge that the churches have not always been welcoming to the women of abortion. Yet such abuses ought not keep women from coming to the faith community for healing.

To trust the invitation of the Pope to repentance requires courage. There must be a willingness to move from denial to acknowledgment, from suspicion to a surrender of those defenses which frustrate grace. For ultimately the call to trust is grounded in the promises of the Father of Mercies. This is the same God and Father who sent his only Son for our salvation. This is the God to whom Jesus teaches us to pray as our loving Father. This is the same God who spreads a table before us. We can trust that the God who does all these, and infinitely more, is *faithful.* The long history of Israel, the sending of Jesus, and the ministry of the Church is testimony that God never goes back on his word or forgets the work of his hands. God is ever mindful of our need; he hears the cries of our wounded hearts. And God continually sends his amazing grace to heal the women of abortion.

Sacrament of Reconciliation

The call to repentance only makes sense, will only be accepted, if the God of Jesus is "the Father of Mercies." And this is exactly what Jesus came to reveal. From the dramatic opening of his public ministry in Galilee with Jesus bringing "good news to the poor, liberty to captives, sight to the blind and release to prisoners" (Lk 4:18-19), he is seen as the Compassion of God. Jesus comes to search for the lost; for those who have traveled to a distant land; and for those who have died to the hope of ever starting over. It is to these in his ministry that Jesus extends mercy, enjoys table fellowship, and proclaims a heavenly rejoicing to celebrate the homecoming of the Father's prodigals.

God's mercy is not frozen in time or confined to a specific

geographical area. Jesus entrusts the ministry of reconciliation to the Church. The Apostle Paul brought the Gospel of Reconciliation through his ministry: "...God was reconciling the world to himself in Christ, not counting their trespasses against them, and entrusting to us the message of reconciliation. So we are ambassadors for Christ, as if God were appealing through us. We implore you on behalf of Christ, be reconciled to God" (2 Cor 5:19-20). Hence, an essential work of the Church is healing. The Church is to continue to search out the lost, welcome home the wayward, and celebrate at the rebirth of one who was once dead because of sin. One of the most profound moments in the life and ministry of the Church occurs when these words are proclaimed, "Your sins are forgiven in the name of the Lord Jesus. Go in peace."

The Catholic Church celebrates seven sacraments which serve as encounters with the Trinity from early life outside the womb (Baptism), to the last of life (Anointing of the Sick), as well as the significant moments of vocation (Marriage, Holy Orders) and the need to be healed and sustained in facing the challenges of living Christ each day (Reconciliation and Eucharist). The Church terms Anointing of the Sick and Reconciliation sacraments of *healing*. Jesus is the Divine Physician who cares for the whole person, body and soul. Jesus healed the physically impaired and forgave sins. The forgiving of sins by Jesus continues through the Sacrament of Reconciliation. The Church forgives sins *in the name of Jesus* and welcomes the forgiven back in the community of faith.

The Pope invites the women of abortion to come and know the Father of Mercies through the Sacrament of Reconciliation. The fruit of such an encounter is forgiveness and peace. Yes, abortion is a terrible wrong. Yes, an innocent human life was lost by the decision of the mother. All of this can be honestly faced in order that the wound in one's heart can be healed. Eager to meet the women of abortion is the Father of Mercies who sent Jesus to forgive sins, and who continues such forgiveness through the sacramental ministry of Reconciliation. John Paul II is echoing the words of the Apostle Paul: "Be reconciled to God" (2 Cor 5:20).

The Question of Excommunication

At the beginning of our reflections we met Julie who was quite angry over the "e" word — excommunication. It seems that the Church talks a good game of forgiveness, healing, and reconciliation, but at the end of the day we must return to the same old punitive, legalistic Church. Sure, the Pope is issuing special words to the women of abortion, but there is that little thing called "Canon Law." And Canon Law expressly states that, "One who procures a successful abortion incurs an automatic excommunication" (Canon 1398).

The reaction of Julie to this Canon is not surprising given our cultural disposition toward law in general, and especially Church law. Our culture clearly advocates a whole cluster of values — autonomy, privacy, and individualism — which sees Church law as oppressive and punitive. On the surface there seems to be a real contradiction between law and love, canons and compassion, rules and reconciliation. However, on closer inspection we see the moral *and* pastoral importance of Canon Law, especially in the instance of abortion.

The Church is both a *human* organization as well as a *divine* mystery founded by Jesus Christ. As a social organization of vast proportions there is the need for law. The law is in place, developed and refined over centuries, to insure order, justice, and the good of the *whole* community. In the absence of law there would be chaos. Church law relates to the entire life of the community of faith in its morality (code), its fundamental beliefs (creed), and in its worship (cult). The law is in place as a protector of these essential components of community life. As such, the law must at times impose sanctions and penalties in order to safeguard these fundamentals of the community. The law must draw *boundaries* concerning what is acceptable and unacceptable. There comes a time when the boundaries are so severely violated by a person's conduct or belief that they must be formally removed from the ongoing life of the community. However, the use of penalties, sanctions, and excommunication serve as measures of last resort. The Church tries by other means to restore the person back to community life. Only if the individual refuses such overtures must the Church, for the good of the whole community, impose more drastic measures.

The use of automatic excommunication is done for two interrelated reasons: the well-being of the community and the healing of the individual. Abortion is often presented as a *private* act. The Church does not share this understanding. For abortion involves the woman, the unborn child, the father, perhaps both families, the abortion provider, society as a whole, and the Church as the Nuptial Body of Christ. Hence abortion is anything but private. It is one of the most social of actions. As such the question of the common good comes into focus. The Church teaches that the killing of innocent human life in the womb is such a gross violation of respect for life that the only recourse is excommunication. It would be a scandal, and endanger the spiritual well-being of the community, for the Church to ignore abortion or trivialize its effects.

At the same time the Church is ever mindful of the needs of the woman who has an abortion. How can the Church be concerned about the woman and at the very same time impose the penalty of automatic excommunication? The answer to this seeming contradiction lies in the Church's *intention* for imposing excommunication. Namely, the conversion of the one excommunicated. In other words, excommunication is imposed with a *medicinal* intent. That is, the Church wants the person to turn from sin and be healed. Excommunication is a radical wake-up call to the individual that a terrible wrong has been done. This wrong is so contrary to the life of the community, and so endangers the soul of the offender, that this radical step must be taken. The Church does this in the hope that the person will come to his or her senses and return to the Father of Mercies.

It must be kept in mind that even in the case of automatic excommunication for abortion, a significant number of conditions are listed by Canon Law which would excuse or mitigate liability. These conditions are listed in Canons 1322 and 1323: lack of prior warning; being under sixteen years old; ignorance that a law is being violated; physical force; grave fear, unless the act is intrinsically evil (abortion); self-defense or defense of another; and lack of reason. Also Canon 1324 recognizes that mitigating circumstances can be present which reduce the applicability of a penalty: impaired reason (alcohol/drugs); acting out of passion; over 16 but under 18 years of age; grave fear or grave inconvenience; unjust or grave provocation; being unaware of the penalty attached to a law; and lack of full imputability.

The above extensive lists of factors which remove or mitigate the application of a penalty clearly indicate the Church is *not* in a mood to rush to judgment. In fact, the Church does all that is morally sound, yet sensitive to the complexity of human behavior, in order to do what is just. The Church goes on to indicate that if *any* of the above factors are present the individual is not liable to the automatic penalty (Canon 1324). The Church is saying in effect that it is very rare to find a situation in which the penalty of automatic excommunication would apply to a woman who has an abortion. In order to fall under the penalty of automatic excommunication the woman who obtains an abortion would have to do so with full knowledge, deliberation, intention, and be free from any circumstances which might prevent or mitigate the penalty. Again, such would be quite rare.

The rarity of finding such a woman does not mean that abortion is not a terrible evil or that the Church is powerless to confront abortion. A whole series of Canons provide for Church authorities to respond to abortion through various penances, warnings, or corrections (Canons 1339-1340). None of this should surprise us if we keep in mind that the reason for various penalties and sanctions is the return of the offender. The Church wants the woman to come home and not be driven to despair. The prudent use of penalties can be a way of providing a bridge to the women of abortion. Dialogue and teaching can commence.

The goal of such dialogue and teaching, prompted by a prudent use of penalties, is to help the woman come to the Sacrament of Reconciliation. In many dioceses the priest is given the faculty to remit the penalty of excommunication and pronounce sacramental absolution. Even if abortion is reserved to the bishops, the confessor may provide absolution if he believes harm will come to the woman if she waits. At some later period (usually within a month) absolution can be given by the bishop or the faculty extended to the confessor. If this is not done, the penalty may fall back in place. It is very important that the confessor assign a fitting penance to the woman. The performance of such a penalty gives evidence of contrition, provides reparation to the extent possible, and offers a way of overcoming any scandal. The use of an appropriate penance is *not* for the punishment of the woman but a way to indicate the serious nature of abortion, to respect the woman's need to overcome guilt by reparation, and to serve as an important expression of integrating the woman back into the community. Rather than seeking to drive women out of the Church, Canon Law and pastoral practice join forces to welcome the women of abortion into the healing love of the Father of Mercies.

A Priest To Turn To

We close this reflection much as we began, with the story of Julie. It is not her anger, a seeming inability to form a committed relationship, or her fatalistic view of life that commands our attention. In the midst of all these negatives there is a ray of hope, "There was a priest I used to talk to...." Yes, he was reassigned. Yes, she lost contact with him. No, she is not presently talking to a priest, *but* there is hope. There is hope that another such priest will cross Julie's path and a dialogue may begin again. There is hope that she might actually come to that place in her life where *she* seeks out such a priest. Nothing is beyond hope with God's grace.

The mere fact that Julie, with all her negatives, still talked to a priest indicates just how important the priest can be in the healing of the women of abortion. Women are looking for those priests who understand, not just theology, but who understand *them.* Women of abortion are looking for priests who are strong enough to be kind. In the words of the Letter to the Hebrews: "...we have a great high priest who passed through the heavens, Jesus, the Son of God.... Every high priest is taken among men.... He is able to deal patiently with the ignorant and erring, for *he himself* is beset by weakness and so, for this reason, must make sin offerings for *himself* as well as for the people" (Heb 5:1-3).

I asked Julie what was so special about her priest that moved her to speak with him.

"There wasn't anything really special," answered Julie with a slight shake of her head, "I mean he was an ordinary kind of guy if you know what I mean. I knew he was a priest but he could talk to me without preaching all the time."

I wanted to know if Julie ever talked about her abortion. "Not really," said Julie as she looked at her nervously moving hands, "but I always had the feeling he knew. But it didn't stop him from acknowledging me. I had the impression that he wanted *me* to bring up the abortion. I never did."

The above conversation with Julie took place about three months ago. Since then she has returned to Mass ("not on a regular basis," she admits), likes the pastor, and is even "playing with the idea of confession." It would not surprise me if Julie does indeed receive the Sacrament of Reconciliation.

Julie is in the midst of a profound struggle. I think she'll win. Her biggest support comes from the Father of Mercies.

REFLECTION 5

Nothing is Definitively Lost

WITHIN THE PAST YEAR LORRAINE HAD an abortion. The wound
is still fresh in her heart. She is in her mid-twenties
and works as a paralegal in a small law office. Lorraine
became involved with an older man she met through
her work. Neither of them had any intention of
getting married. The reality of a child was totally out of
the question. "At the time," said Lorraine, "the only way
out was abortion. At least that's the way it seemed to us."
She still sees the aborted baby's father. "But there's
nothing there," says Lorraine with more than a twinge of
sadness. "There's like an unspoken agreement,"
continues Lorraine, "that we don't bring up the baby or
what happened." Even though Lorraine and the
father do not speak about the abortion, this doesn't
keep her from wondering what might have been. "I
can't help but wonder about the baby," says Lorraine,
"and all the things we might have done... all the
things we won't do."
The wound left by abortion manifests itself uniquely for
each woman. For Lorraine there is a deep sense of loss.
There is the need to offer some kind of explanation;
some kind of apology to the child.
"I only wish I could explain what happened," says
Lorraine. "I want my baby to know that I...." Her voice
trails off into a silence which seems to acknowledge the
futility of such thoughts.
The wound that is so painful in Lorraine's heart comes

43

from the belief that death is the *final* word. She believes
that with the decision to abort her child, also aborted
was any chance for reconciliation. Lorraine believes only
silence, loss, and pain remain. She wonders when life
will return to normal.
"I guess my wanting to move on is just another example
of my being selfish," said Lorraine.
What Lorraine is calling "a return to normal" or "a
selfish need to move on," is in reality a cry for
reconciliation with her child.
Pope John Paul II's words respond to such a cry.

A very basic way of coping with loss is to share the experience. We seek out others who have experienced a similar loss
in the hope of finding some understanding. We seek out those
who can offer us a word of comfort or some sign they feel our
pain. From losing the big game to losing a major business
account, a kind word or an arm draped across the shoulders
by a friend helps put things in perspective. The enormity of
the loss and its subsequent pain become manageable when
shared with those who understand. A loss that is not shared
only increases our pain and isolation.

Abortion and Loss

The experience of loss associated with abortion is often
one not shared. As mentioned previously, there is little or no
support for such loss due to abortion. Society views abortion
as a private choice by women who calculate what is in their
best interest. Abortion frees women to realize all their desired
goals unencumbered by nature — pregnancy. Hence, there
is little or no social support for one to feel loss over the death
of one's unborn child. Often when it comes to dealing with

loss by turning to one's family there is more pain than comfort. From embarrassment to banishment, from silence to stigma, abortion carries an intense pain resulting from its special sense of loss.

The special sense of loss associated with abortion goes beyond the refusal of society and family to offer support. The women of abortion experience loss due to *their decision*. It was within *their control* to continue the life of their unborn child. Abortion was not the result of some bad breaks or act of nature; a decision was made by the woman (the child's mother) and she must now face the consequences. When all the rationalizations fall away, and the ideology of our culture of death is exposed as a lie, the woman is left to face the weight of her action. The loss of life has taken something out of her as well.

With a loss we always hope for a comeback or second chance. Yet abortion is so final. The life of the unborn child is ended. In our highly secular culture death is the *absolute* final reality. It is easy to see how despair can take root in one's heart. If we live for *this* life only, then that life in the womb was of short duration and the wound in the heart of the woman remains. What was done cannot be undone. There are no second chances. There is no opportunity for reconciliation. Death closes the door.

Life Is Not Ended

Into such despair comes John Paul II with his healing message of hope: "You will come to understand that nothing is definitively lost.…"

There is no offer of a quick fix or cheap grace. There is a *process* that requires time and understanding if healing is to take place. We must look beyond the surface of things, beyond the horizon of the immediate, in order to see God's steadfast love at work. Yes, the heart of the woman who had an abortion is filled with guilt, pain, and a deep sense of loss. Yes, the immediate reality is death. However, in the midst of all these effects of sin is saving grace. When the reality of loss is most acutely felt, when despair's grip on the heart is most intense, God is present re-creating, restoring, and offering hope. For God is committed to life and brings to himself *all* that is good. While this unborn child has passed from *this* life, such a passage *continues* into the life of God. Nothing of value falls outside of God's providential care. The unborn child is not definitively lost.

Pope John Paul II is reminding us of that consoling dimension of our faith called the Communion of Saints. We Catholics believe that at death "life is changed, not ended." The dead are not only the dearly departed but also the newly arrived. This is especially the case with the "modern innocents" — the unborn who are the victims of abortion. These children now rest in the peace of the Lord. In the words of the book of Revelation, "He will wipe every tear from their eyes, and there shall be no more death or mourning, wailing or pain, for the old order has passed away" (Rv 21:4).

The Communion of Saints not only assures us that those who die in the Lord are at peace, but that we can still *communicate* with our loved ones through *prayer*. And *they* can be an advocate for us before the throne of God. This reciprocal relationship in prayer is contained in the *Catechism of the Catholic Church*: "Our prayer for them is capable not only of helping them, but also of making their intercessions for us effective" (No. 958). The victory of Jesus on the Cross breaks the power of death. We can continue to love, honor, and aid our loved ones through prayer. Those women who chose abortion can be assured that the conversation can continue. Your child wants to hear what you have to say. You are not speaking into a void or the empty heavens. God gathers to himself these children of abortion and protects them with his love.

Reconciliation

"I only wish I had the chance to explain things," says Susan who had an abortion almost a year ago. "I want my baby to know how sorry I am," she continues, "and how much I wish things had been different."

Part of the pain the women of abortion experience is not just the loss of their child but the loss of having a final goodbye. Especially there is the need to express regret to the child. There is the need to know that forgiveness is possible. There is the need to know that the child is in some better place.

John Paul II is telling women all of these are possible: you can express your regret to your child who is now at peace in the Lord. But just as important, you can be assured that reconciliation is possible. For those who live in the Lord, in his love, there is perfect understanding. In the most profound and consoling of thoughts, the Pope is saying to the women of abortion: You will see your child again. Yes, *both* of you can be reunited in the Lord's presence in heaven. What you hoped for is not beyond hope. There will be a meeting in that life to come. You will be able to tell your story. You will be able to ask forgiveness. Face to face with your child, you will hear the words that are only now a distant hope. Once again the Pope is counseling against despair. He is inviting women to trust in the promises of that God whose love saves all that is good and heals the wounds of abortion.

Lorraine Revisited

Lorraine understandably wants to return to "normal" and "move on" with her life. On a purely psychological level no doubt this is considered a healthy goal, a sign of recovery. But John Paul II moves beyond the psychological into the realm of the spiritual. The Pope is offering women like Lorraine more than a return to life the way it was. The Pope is challenging women to look forward and see life the way it could be. Specifically, the Pope does not want the women of abortion to be trapped in their past. Accepting their past, refusing to give in to despair, living with hope, the women of abortion can become "eloquent defenders of everyone's right to life."

John Paul II is saying that the women of abortion can become the women who respect life. Their own experience with abortion can become a source of guidance for other women. It is to the invitation to become "eloquent defenders of everyone's right to life" that we now turn.

Reflection 6

Defenders of Life

SYLVIA IS IN HER EARLY FORTIES and at a place in her life where she never thought she would be. "When I was in my mid-twenties I had an abortion," she begins, "and at first I believed it was the right answer for my situation." However, as time went on Sylvia came to see that abortion was not a solution. She experienced a rather lengthy and severe period of depression. In order to cope, Sylvia "threw herself into work" in the hope that she "could put the situation behind me." Yet the hyper-activity and exhaustion did not bring relief.

Sylvia's job performance began to suffer. "I never used drugs or alcohol," she said, "my addiction was work. But rather than bring me peace, it became a source of increased stress. I almost lost my job." Sylvia was fortunate to have a spiritually understanding boss. When things reached a crisis stage at work, Sylvia's boss called her in for a conference. "I really thought I was going to get fired," said Sylvia with a smile that comes from being fortunately surprised. "I was shocked that we spent most of the time talking about what was going on inside of me. My supervisor was a religious person. Although we weren't of the same faith, I am a Catholic, he spoke about some spiritual matters. I hadn't thought about my faith for quite some time."

The fact that Sylvia had an abortion did not make the topic of religion appealing. Yet as the weeks went by Sylvia couldn't shake the feeling that she should give her faith a new look. "I started slowly," said Sylvia. "You

know. I began to pray. I showed up at Mass every now
and then."
More than a year after her conversation with her boss,
Sylvia made an appointment to see the priest in her
parish. "From the few times I heard him preach," said
Sylvia, "I felt I could talk to him. We talked about things
in general. It was really good for me. I felt I was on the
way to some peace." Finally, Sylvia spoke with her pastor
about her abortion.
"I wanted to get things right with the Church," said
Sylvia, "and I just felt it was time to confess. It wasn't easy
but I've never regretted *that* decision."
In the subsequent years Sylvia has become, what Pope
John Paul II has termed, a most "eloquent defender of
life." She does not do this in a very visible way. "I don't
attend meetings or march at clinics," says Sylvia, "but
what I do is pray. I pray for my child. I pray for all the
children who will be aborted. I pray for women who
have had abortions. I pray that women who are thinking
about abortion will make a decision for life."

In addition to being a fundamental constitutional right,
abortion is also presented as a *private choice*. Abortion is an issue for women only. No one, not even the father, has the right
to offer any input in the final decision. Abortion is about the
woman's body and her right to do what she wants with her
body. When it comes to reproductive rights they belong with
absolute exclusivity to the woman who makes her choice.

This talk of privacy, rights, and the freedom to make decisions about one's body plays well in our culture. However,
John Paul II counters this litany of "values" with a set of "virtues" that emphasizes solidarity, community, responsibility,
and an authentic freedom guided by truth. Above all, the Pope
rejects out of hand the fallacy that abortion is a private choice.

Social Nature of Abortion

Abortion is never a private choice involving only the woman. Regardless of the Supreme Court's dismissal of the unborn as "a non-person in the full constitutional sense of the term" (translation: not entitled to basic human rights and constitutional protections such as due process and protection by the state of innocent human life), abortion is the killing of a unique human being. Furthermore, the decision concerning abortion affects the father, one's family and friends, one's current and future children, future relationships, the medical community, and society as a whole. From this extensive and complex cluster of social entities it is clear that abortion extends beyond the private choice of the mother.

John Paul II goes further than merely describing the social dimension of abortion. He also speaks to women about the importance of "the friendly and expert help and advice of other people." These significant others can be of great benefit in helping the women of abortion in their journey toward healing and reconciliation.

The women of abortion often find themselves alone, abandoned by a culture, industry, and significant others who withdraw during and after the abortion. Women are assured abortion is simple and of no lasting consequence. However, when this does *not* turn out to be the case, women are left to fend for themselves. Such is the cold reality of the privacy of abortion. Such a privacy becomes a prison in which women feel unable to speak of their loss and share their pain.

The Pope tells women this isolation and loneliness need not be the case. The women of abortion *do* have friends who want what is best for them. Friends who want to walk with them in their journey from the wounded heart to a heart healed through reconciliation. The fear of rejection and condemna-

tion is strong. Too often women feel as if abortion is the ultimate sin for which there is no forgiveness. This fear drives
women into a deeper silence and despair. The love of individual Christians, plus the faith community as a whole, can
break through fear. The Gospel of Life is for the women of
abortion and can empower them to become witnesses for respecting life. The Church, entrusted with the Gospel of Life,
is in solidarity with women and their aborted children in order to effect a reconciliation.

The medical community in general, and the psychiatric
profession in particular, have much to offer the women of
abortion. To be specific, the women of abortion must be told
the truth about abortion. Their pain, as a result of abortion,
must not be trivialized. Women know in the deepest sense that
the life within is more than tissue or a mass of cells. Women
know that their pain and sense of loss are real. They mourn
over a lost life because of their decision. The guilt and shame
they feel must not be assigned to some other cause. Women
know the gravity of their decision. They must be helped to face
their decision in order for true healing to take place.

Many in the psychiatric profession are not alert to the
possibility that depression may be the result of an abortion.
E. Joanne Angelo, M.D., who has years of clinical experience
with women who have had abortions, attributes this inatten-
tion to a number of factors: Firstly, women simply do not talk
about their abortions. Shame and guilt keep them silent. Sec-
ondly, there is a time lag between the abortion and the woman
seeking help for her depression. This delay can throw the
therapist off track. It is not uncommon for this delay to range
between eight and ten years. Thirdly, the therapist often looks
to other negative factors such as alcohol, drug, and sexual
abuse in order to account for the depression. And finally,
when women try to initially share their grief and shame they

are often dismissed as unimportant. The inability of women to find someone who will listen and understand can drive women into a deeper despair. They turn to drugs and/or alcohol. And an increase in suicidal thoughts is not uncommon.

The women of abortion need therapists who are able to listen to their stories. Such listening comes without the need to give all the answers, clarify all issues, and heal all wounds. Women need to be able to express their pain in an unfiltered way. Women need to tell their stories without being rejected or given a moral sermon. At the same time, women need to be helped to face their decision, the death of their child, and to be given the hope of reconciliation. The therapist can be of great help by allowing the woman to express the images she may have formed of her child. The therapist may help the woman give her child a name and even share some of the conversations she had with her child. The therapist may be able to help the woman formulate images of her child now at peace and beyond suffering. If the woman has a set of religious convictions, these can be very helpful in moving to reconciliation. If appropriate, the therapist can help the woman turn to her Church or place of worship. Psychiatry and religion can work together in providing the woman with a wholistic approach to healing.

Painful Experience

Abortion is not the simple, pain-free "procedure" it is usually portrayed to be. There is often physical pain which results from abortion; from abdominal pain to bleeding, the woman is reminded of what has occurred. There is also the emotional and psychological pain which results from a deep sense of loss and a grief which few understand. There is the moral pain which comes from having made the decision to abort one's baby. The shame and guilt are real and not the result of psychological or emotional immaturity. And there is the terrible sense of loneliness which comes to the women of abortion who cannot share the wound in their hearts.

Our culture does its best to assure women that all these dimensions of pain will soon pass. Given enough time, therapy, and distractions a woman will soon be back to her old self. Yet women come to see that such is not the case. In fact, the passage of time only makes the pain more acute. Women come to see that abortion was not the answer to their situation. The unwanted or unplanned pregnancy is not "fixed" by terminating the life of the unborn child.

Our faith, very much counter-cultural, assures women that their pain and suffering can be redemptive. Suffering need not be denied or quickly anesthetized. Suffering can be a great teacher; in fact, some of our most important truths are learned only in the school of suffering. To be sure, we do not seek it out as a good in itself. But suffering comes to each of us offering an opportunity to grow in love. This is especially true when we join our sufferings to those of Jesus. The meaning of the suffering changes. It is no longer destructive but redemptive; not isolating but invites solidarity, and not enslaving but liberates us for deeper ways of caring for others. The suffering experienced by the women of abortion can become a bridge from the past into a future respecting life.

Defenders of Life

Sylvia, a woman who had an abortion, became what John Paul II has termed an "eloquent defender of everyone's right to life." Her eloquent defense of life was not done in a highly visible manner. She chose the ministry of prayer. While not as public as some forms of defending life, the power of prayer should never be underestimated. For in the end the goal of all pro-life activities is a change of heart and culture. We want to help bring about the civilization of life and love. The culture of death's defeat will require many forms of ministry. The many gifts and blessings of the Holy Spirit must come together in love. No one who truly ministers on behalf of respecting life need feel their gifts are unimportant. All people of good will can come together on behalf of life.

Barbara is more of an activist. She had two abortions in her twenties. She had what she terms "a conversion experience" after speaking to a nun who taught her years ago in high school.

"There was just something in the way Sister talked to me," said Barbara, "that made me want to get myself right with the Lord." For the past several years Barbara has been active in the pro-life movement in her state as well as her Church parish. Barbara usually gives a public testimony about her past and the way "the Lord has worked to turn my life around. It's as if there were two different people."

Barbara is especially effective with young people. She is often invited to speak at local high schools about the importance of chastity and the lessons she learned from her abortions. Barbara has toyed with the idea of "doing something political" but for now she is committed "to sharing my story in the hope it will help others."

For both Sylvia and Barbara, as well as countless other women who have had abortions, the grace of God is at work. At the center of the Gospel of Life is the message of God's unbounded love for all creation. God is the God of life. Yes, there are women who have participated in the culture of death. However, the civilization of life and love is stronger.

God will never give up in searching for those who are lost, lonely, and in pain. There is always the hope of conversion, reconciliation, and healing the wound of abortion. What God has done for Sylvia and Barbara, God can do for each woman affected by abortion.

Your Commitment to Life

D IANE BY HER OWN ADMISSION HAS HAD "several" abortions. "You would think I would have learned," offered Diane with a shake of her head, "but it almost became the thing to do when I got pregnant."

Her various abortions began in her late teens and extended into her early twenties. Each time Diane promised herself she wouldn't have another abortion. Yet each time she turned to abortion as "a way to make things right."

Diane had been friends with a group of people who played "fast and loose with all kinds of stuff. We did drugs, alcohol, and it just seemed that sex was part of the package."

Diane began to see the toll all this was taking on her. She resolved to break away and put her life on track. But how? Diane was living with her mother. Fortunately Diane's mother received a job offer in another part of the state. She accepted the offer and both of them moved. It was a new job for Diane's mother and the possibility of a new beginning for Diane.

Sure enough, Diane made some new friends through her part-time job. Two of these new friends were active in their church and invited Diane along. She was reluctant at first but soon began to feel welcome. Over the course of time Diane began to experience a slow inward change, "a conversion," in which she was deeply ashamed of her past; especially the part having to do with abortion.

However, she finally worked up enough courage to
share her story with her friends. They encouraged her to
talk with the Pastor. Again, with great reluctance she did
so. To her surprise she didn't feel condemnation but "a
real peace that I hadn't felt since I don't know when."
Subsequently Diane met a church member, Robert,
whom she fell in love with and married. Unfortunately
Diane and Robert have been unable to have children.
"The abortions I had...," said Diane as her voice trailed
off. "It's the price I have to pay... and Robert too."
One day Robert proposed adoption. "I had never
thought of a child that wasn't my own," said Diane, "but
more and more I liked the idea. Robert was so positive
about the whole thing."
After much thought and prayer Diane and Robert
decided to go ahead and they were blessed with a
beautiful, healthy baby. "I couldn't imagine life without
Robert and Stacy."

Spes contra spes. Hope against hope.

Unfortunately not all, not nearly all, of the stories of the
women of abortion turn out so well. The women of abortion
often live with the feeling that abortion is the ultimate, unforgivable sin against God. These women can relate to the
word of Cain: "My sin is too great to be forgiven." Too often
they feel marked in a way that makes them wanderers in search
of hope and healing. We will never know how many women
go to the Lord not having found that reconciliation which
brings peace.

Because there are so many women who have had abortions, Pope John Paul II has offered his special word. Just when
despair is closest and hope is swallowed up in the dark hole
of resignation, the Pope boldly declares that the women of
abortion can show a "commitment to life." Yes, you had an
abortion. Yes, it was wrong. Yes, there is a wound in your heart.
But all that need never be the last word. Death can give way

to life. The abandonment of the unborn can now be a commitment to *all* life. Your painful past can be healed and you can be a source of wisdom and strength for others.

Yet there is an inner voice which says to the women of abortion: "There has been so much hurt. Any talk of forgiveness is simply a way out of a tough situation. You simply cannot walk away from this terrible wrong."

Powerful stuff to be sure. However, the Pope will not be discouraged from what he believes is our mission on behalf of the Gospel of Life: we must build the civilization of life and love *together*. Yes *all* of us must bring what we have to the effort. The women of abortion bring their wounded hearts, pain, and experience that abortion is *not* a solution. They know first hand the tragedy of abortion. They bring a truth so real the hair on our necks stands at attention.

A Tale of Two Women

The ministry of Jesus to those who were considered sinners is one of truth and hope. Jesus did not shy away from confronting the reality of sin and the need to call sinners to conversion. He could do this so effectively because his ministry was grounded in love and respect. Jesus knew that the power of love was greater than the love of power over others. The crowds sensed in Jesus one who lived among them with authority, that is, the authority of one who spoke the truth in love. Sinners could face their past because they knew the future was one of hope and not condemnation. They could acknowledge their sins because his love drove out all fear. They could dare to become a new creation because of the word spoken by the One who makes all things new.

The Gospels contain the stories of two women: one with

a name, Mary Magdalene, and the other nameless, the woman who anoints the feet of Jesus. Both women speak across the centuries to women who have had abortions. They speak about the burdens of a sinful past. They speak about meeting Jesus and being given a new beginning. Above all, these two women speak to the women of abortion about hope. Yes, hope against hope.

Women were attracted to Jesus; and he to them. Of special concern to Jesus were women who had troubled pasts and were rejected as sinners. One such woman remains nameless, but her example of love will endure as long as Scripture itself. Specifically, it is the woman who anoints the feet of Jesus.

We meet this woman in the Gospel of Luke (7:31-50). This will not surprise us if we keep in mind that Luke's story of Jesus centers on the compassion of God. Jesus comes to announce the year of the Lord's favor to the poor, to sinners, and to the rejected. A special place is reserved for women, sinners, publicans, and all who are open to grace. Jesus is the Divine Physician who comes to heal the brokenhearted.

It seems that a leading Pharisee gives a dinner and invites Jesus. Yet it is an uninvited woman who steals the show. For she anoints Jesus' feet with her tears and perfumed oil. She dries his feet with her hair. The Pharisee, Simon, is taken back because this woman is known to all as a sinner. Jesus should have nothing to do with her. She will contaminate him. To the surprise of those in attendance, Jesus rebukes Simon. Why? Because he didn't show Jesus the basics of hospitality. It was this woman who showed love. Jesus says that because of her great love her sins are forgiven. Notice love is prior to the forgiveness of sins. The greatness of her capacity to love prepares her *to accept* forgiveness. Jesus pronounces her sins forgiven and sends her in peace.

The story of the woman who anoints the feet of Jesus is

relevant to women who have had abortions. The women of abortion know what it means to be among the uninvited and scorned. The modern abortion culture, while seeming to be understanding, really trivializes the experience of women (loss, guilt, shame). Women are not invited to go public with their feelings of loss at the death of their unborn child. The culture does not allow for women to express remorse and seek reconciliation. Just the opposite. Women can only find a place at the table if they express gratitude for the "right" to an abortion.

Not only the culture but also members of the Church can be just as unwelcoming to the women of abortion. Women can be made to feel that they contaminate everything they touch. Some Church members denounce abortion with such vigor that there is no hospitality shown to the women themselves. The impression given is that abortion is the unforgivable sin. Women can easily give in to despair and face the future without hope.

Both the culture and the attitude of these individuals are rejected by Jesus. There remains in the woman who anoints Jesus the capacity for love. This is connected to her forgiveness. She never stops loving; hence she is open to accept forgiveness. She is not locked into despair, self-hatred, self-pity, or the false evaluations of others. Love drives out all these fears and opens her to forgiveness and peace. The Pope is saying the very same thing: Women of abortion do not stop living. Do not give in to despair. Do not let fear imprison you and prevent you from accepting the forgiving words of Jesus. Women of abortion, you must love, accept forgiveness, and you will know peace. Women of abortion, by your love you can be an example of commitment to life. The forgiving words of Jesus make this possible. You can anoint other women who face an unwanted pregnancy with the wisdom gained from your painful experience.

No woman has experienced the healing power of Jesus' love more than Mary Magdalene (Jn 20:11-18). In the Gospel of Luke there is mention that at the end of one of Jesus' extended periods of ministry he enjoyed the hospitality of some women who accompanied him. Among these women was one named Mary Magdalene "from whom seven devils had gone out" (Lk 8:1-3). This possessed woman had been released by Jesus and she is now a disciple offering hospitality. Jesus broke the grip of the past with all its demons. Mary was now part of Jesus' ministry to others who needed healing.

Mary's role in the life and ministry of Jesus reaches its high point on that first Easter morning. In the Gospel of John we find Mary "weeping beside the tomb" (Jn 20:11). Also present are two angels who want to know why she is weeping. Mary believes that someone took the body of Jesus and she won't be able to minister to his body. She is asked once again why she is weeping. This time it is by someone she believes to be the gardener. This unknown person calls Mary by name and she comes to recognize that it is Jesus. Her recognition is imperfect. She calls Jesus "Teacher"; yet he is more. Mary tries to cling to Jesus but she is told by him, "Go to my brothers and tell them 'I am ascending to my Father and your Father, to my God and your God!'" (Jn 20:17). Mary goes to the disciples with the proclamation, "I have seen the Lord!" (Jn 20:18).

Here is Mary Magdalene, a woman who was possessed by seven devils, being the first one to meet the risen Lord on that first Easter. Yes, it was imperfect and not without flaws. But what is crucial is that Jesus sends her to announce his resurrection and ascension. She gives us an understanding of who Jesus is. For Mary tells the disciples she has seen "the Lord." Jesus is no longer just a Teacher, but the Lord of Life who gave Mary back her life. She now goes forth to proclaim the Gospel.

Your Commitment to Life

If we fast-forward from the time of Jesus to the present moment of John Paul II we find a splendid consistency; namely, God's grace can write straight with the crooked lines of our lives. God fills in the rough spots and brings forth new life in the most arid of conditions. What Jesus did for the unknown woman who anointed him and Mary Magdalene, he wants to do for women who have had abortions. That is, Jesus drives out the demons of the past and offers a new beginning. No doubt this unknown woman, and Mary, never dreamed of what the future held. No doubt they felt that today and tomorrow would be like yesterday. However, they met Jesus. And they were ready to accept the invitation to be healed, forgiven, and minister to others.

In our next reflection we will examine some specific ways in which women who have had abortions can promote the Gospel of Life. There is a trauma after abortion; likewise, there is a ministry on behalf of life open to women. It is to this ministry that we now turn.

REFLECTION 8

A New Way

B EA IS IN HER LATE FIFTIES. Years ago "before it was legal and
out in the open" she had an abortion. Bea lived in a
small town so she had to leave in order to get the
abortion. Her mother arranged for the procedure and
kept it a secret from her father.
"It was a very bad time," said Bea in a tone which
indicated there was still a residue of pain. "I was so
scared and ashamed. My mother was so upset."
Bea graduated from high school and worked in various
local businesses. As the years went by Bea moved from
that small town to a large city in the mid-west. She has
no children and never married.
"I saw some of the things my mother went through," said
Bea. "And I didn't want that for me. At times I think I
made a mistake. Who knows?"
Leaving aside her personal life, Bea is happily involved
in some part-time volunteer work. Specifically, Bea
works with adolescents and young adults who are facing
difficult situations involving pregnancy.
"I never really thought of myself in any kind of religious
way," says Bea with a faint smile. "But several years ago
my pastor gave a sermon in which he talked about the
need to be of service. He said that Jesus wanted us to
help others. I left church trying to think how I could
help others." Several weeks passed but nothing came to
mind.
"One day I was talking to a friend at work," said Bea,

"and she asked if her daughter could speak with me
about a problem. I was a little surprised but said sure."
Bea's friend's daughter was having a difficult time with
her boy friend. From past conversations with Bea this
young woman felt Bea might give her some sound
advice. It seemed to have worked out well.
"It came to me that maybe I could help other women,"
said Bea, "avoid some of my mistakes. Especially I felt I
could help young girls with questions about sex and
about abortion."
Bea still can't believe that she is in the position of
counseling others. "I don't do much," says Bea with a
genuine sense of modesty. "I listen and try my best to tell
them what happened to me. I was wrong about sex at
such an early age. I was definitely wrong about
abortion."
Bea's pastor knows about her past and "is very
supportive of my work with my young ladies." Bea
receives spiritual direction on a regular basis from her
pastor. "I don't want to get in over my head," she says.

John Paul II does not merely extend to women "a special word" which addresses only their private need for healing. The Pope views abortion within the larger context of *culture*. That is, the Pope understands our particular moment in
history as one of real crisis. Today we are faced with the conflict
between the culture of death and the civilization of life and
love. The unique challenge that faces the churches, and all
people of good will, is that of building the civilization of life
and love and dismantling the culture of death. The old labels
of liberal and conservative; democratic, socialist, and repub-
lican; are empty. The decision which confronts each person
is whether one witnesses on behalf of respecting life or sides
with the forces of death (abortion, euthanasia, assisted suicide,
drugs, war, urban violence, neglect of the poor, violence
against minorities and all those at risk, and disregard for the

environment). Contemporary culture exhibits a tremendous technological sophistication and material abundance. However, contemporary culture is spiritually impoverished and morally adrift in relativism, subjectivism, and selfish individualism. The conversion of our contemporary culture calls for a commitment to building the civilization of life and love (respect for all life, the rule of law, respect for human rights, solidarity with the poor, thirsting for justice, extending that ordered freedom which promotes the common good).

In order for us to cooperate with the working of the Holy Spirit for such a cultural conversion, John Paul calls for "a new feminism" and "a new evangelization." In both of these the Pope believes that women are to play an essential role. The women of abortion can offer a tremendous witness in building the civilization of life and love.

A New Feminism

In 1995 the United Nations convened its Fourth World Conference on Women held in Beijing. In preparation for the conference, Pope John Paul II issued a "Letter to Women." This important letter contained the following:

> a greater presence of women in society will prove most valuable, for it will help to manifest the contradictions present when society is organized solely according to the criteria of efficiency and productivity, and it will force systems to be redesigned in a way which favors the process of humanization which marks the 'civilization of love' (No. 4).

With these stirring words John Paul is looking to women to play an essential role in building the civilization of love. The

Pope is looking to women to assert those spiritual and moral values which stand in contrast to a cultural system that values only production, consumption, efficiency, and the bottom line. Women have traditionally been powerful witnesses to those human values which extol family life, solidarity, human dignity, the common good, and the imperative to defend the weak. The ability of women to transform culture is termed by the Pope "a new feminism."

At the heart of this feminism is the proper view of human relationships. That is, "human relations are authentic if they are open to accepting the other person." Such acceptance is not based on some pseudo-tolerance or a contemporary anything-goes approach to life. Rather, accepting the other person is grounded in human dignity. And this dignity flows from being made in the image and likeness of God. The contemporary culture emphasizes "usefulness, strength, intelligence, beauty or health." The "new feminism" respects each person simply because she is human. Each person has dignity and infinite value because of our common origin and destiny in God. Hence, the respect we owe to each person comes not from the ability to achieve but from the sheer fact of existence (*The Gospel of Life*, No. 99).

According to John Paul women are gifted with the ability to "see persons with their hearts." That is, women are blessed with the insight to see and value the uniqueness of each person. Women do not view human beings in terms of consumption and production. Women see the whole person and know that the value of human life cannot be measured in terms of economic or political considerations. Women are especially sensitive to those in need and reach out in love to the neighbor.

Again this call for a "new feminism" by the Pope should not be surprising if we keep in mind his apostolic letter, *The*

Dignity of Women, written in 1988. In that letter John Paul advances what he calls "the feminine genius" which women have exhibited throughout history. By this he means the many and varied ways the Holy Spirit has worked through women in transforming culture through love. Of special significance is the way in which God has *entrusted* to women the gift of life. This sense of being entrusted with the gift of life grounds the moral and spiritual strength of women. The "genius of women" for the sacredness of all human life is crucial for a culture which is so bound to technology, instrumentality, and economic production. Technological culture easily comes to view all life in a utilitarian way:

> In our own time, the success of science and technology make it possible to attain material well-being to a degree hitherto unknown. While this favors some, it pushes others to the edges of society. In this way, unilateral progress can also lead to a gradual *loss of sensitivity for man, that is, for what is essentially human.* In this sense, our time in particular *awaits the manifestation* of that "genius" which belongs to women, and which can ensure sensitivity for human beings in every circumstance: because they are human! — and because "the greatest of these is love" (cf. 1 Cor 13:13). (No. 30)

All of this splendid talk about a "new feminism" and the "genius of women" can seem quite hollow to the women of abortion. After all, haven't their decisions been against the civilization of life and love? Haven't the women of abortion proved that they do not have that love and respect for human life which alone can transform the culture of death? Aren't the women of abortion excluded from seeing "persons with their hearts"?

In response to all of these questions the "special word" of John Paul takes on a great urgency. For the Pope ends his

word to the women of abortion this way: "you will become promoters of a new way of looking at human life." Yes, your decision was wrong. Yes, your abortion is part of the culture of
death. However, your past decision need not prevent you from
helping to build the civilization of life and love. Through reconciliation and healing you can strengthen others who face a
similar decision. Your pain, the wound in your heart, can be
a source of healing for women who feel alone and not understood. Far from being rejected, the Pope is inviting the women
of abortion to promote new ways of respecting life. Women
who have had abortions know that abortion is not the solution. Women who have had abortions know first hand what it
is to be victimized by the abortion industry.

Through your pain and journey to healing you can help
transform our culture. The Pope is calling the women of abortion to help move our culture, obsessed with individualism,
privacy, autonomy and utility, to one which nurtures, empa-
thizes with, and sacrifices for all persons. These qualities of
character reflect the "new feminism" and the "genius of
women." Abortion does *not* eliminate these gifts. With reconciliation comes new ways of respecting life in all its forms.

A New Evangelization

The Gospel of Jesus Christ, the Gospel of Life, is to be
carried to the whole world (Mt 28:16-20). The call to discipleship is the call to be sent with the message that Jesus is Lord
of the living and the dead. Each disciple is sent to live the
Gospel in one's particular situation. Each disciple has a unique
contribution to make on behalf of life. The women of abortion are called to be disciples of the Gospel of Life, to make
their unique contribution.

Pope John Paul II has characterized our culture as one in which a sense of God has been *eclipsed*. That is, contemporary culture is characterized by "materialism, individualism, and hedonism" which promotes the culture of death. Simply put, in our cultural context the primary feature is the death of God. In the place of the living God, modern culture places the imperial, autonomous self seeking its own glory. Such a self operates by those values which see all things in terms of meeting the wants of the isolated self. Things and persons only have value to the extent that they can be used to satisfy one's desires. The self is radically free to construct and reconstruct itself according to the wants of the moment. All relationships are understood totally in terms of utility, productivity, and pleasure.

The culture of death, therefore, is constituted by the death of God. There is an absence of the living presence of God as Creator, Redeemer, and Sanctifier. Life is not a gift but an achievement, a product we construct in our own image and likeness. God is no longer the focus of our individual and cultural life. Life is stripped of its wonder and is understood in merely material categories. There is no sense of transcendence and after-life. The culture of death declares that we live for *this* life only. The windows on that "other dimension" are sealed and shaded over.

John Paul II in his call to a "new evangelization" is challenging us to throw open the sealed windows, recover a sense of wonder in the giftedness of life, and reconnect with the mystery of existence. The Pope is calling us to build the civilization of life and love through *holiness*. It is our change of heart that can help to change the culture. Such an evangelization calls us to respect all of life as gift and to see each person as a living image of God. We are to evangelize, to bring the Gospel of Life to a culture which is spiritually impoverished. We are to announce, with joy and love, the message that all life is sacred. We bear a special obligation toward those who are weak, powerless, and vulnerable. Those whom the culture of death discards, the civilization of life and love makes welcome.

The women of abortion can serve as evangelizers in a special way. For women who have experienced abortion know well the lies of the culture of death. Women know that abortion was not the solution to their pregnancy. The culture of death abandoned women in their pain and loss to fend for themselves. The culture of death trivializes women's sense of loss by a shallow appeal to the rhetoric of reproductive rights, individual choice, and the illusion of complete autonomy.

The women of abortion can serve as evangelizers on behalf of life by accepting their healing and helping others. Women can evangelize in the quiet but effective way of prayer and personal penance. Women can evangelize by accepting the gift of children and promoting family life. Women can witness on behalf of life by adoption, helping the poor, and if possible offering some time to be with the sick and dying. Some women will be more visible through a public testimony, organizing the community on behalf of life, working to change unjust laws and electing pro-life candidates, and still other women will work to change the culture through education and the arts. The common thread that unites these various forms of evangelization is this: all human life is sacred and to be received as *gift*. Such is the foundation of the civilization of life and love.

Accept Your Healing

ENNY HAS BEEN STRUGGLING WITH her abortion for the past two years. The struggle involves her willingness to seek reconciliation and healing. "I know in my head and in my heart that what I did was wrong," acknowledges Jenny. "I wish I had never had an abortion," she continues, "it certainly wasn't the answer." Jenny very much wants "to get back to Church and be a Catholic." However, there is a persistent gap between Jenny's desire for reconciliation and her taking the necessary concrete steps to realize her goal.

"It seems that each time I decide to go see the priest, or talk to someone at the parish, something comes up," said Jenny in a rather fatalistic manner. Jenny, in fact, has made several appointments to see her pastor. Unfortunately she has not kept any of them.

"I have to admit," said Jenny, "that I am nervous about going to see the priest." Yet she goes on to admit that this nervousness is not the result of any harshness she fears from her pastor. "There is simply a kind of hesitation," said Jenny. "I am not sure why."

Jenny continues to profess a desire to return to the sacraments. At the same time she talks about "needing a little more time."

"Maybe I am waiting for that bolt out of the blue" and "wanting a little more encouragement from some friends." Jenny doesn't see any of this as avoidance behavior. In fact, any prolonged discussion of her

situation is usually met with a stern, "don't put any more
pressure on me."
Jenny is sure she will "know when the time is right."
"Besides," says Jenny in a somewhat defensive mode,
"you have to do a lot of this yourself. You have to be
comfortable with what's going on. This is something I'll
have to work at."

It seems like such an easy thing — to accept healing. After
all, who wants to be infirm? Who enjoys pain as a constant com-
panion? A significant part of Jesus' ministry involved healing
the sick. Down through the centuries the Church has stood
in solidarity with those who suffer. Yet as strange as it may seem
there are times when we hold fast to our burdens and make
friends with our demons. There are times when we hold on
to the well-known past rather than venture into the unknown
future.

Jesus encountered those who grew comfortable with their
disability and denied the possibility of being healed. But the
question persists: why do we hesitate at Jesus' invitation to be
healed?

"Do you want to be well?"

The fifth chapter of John's Gospel opens with a decep-
tively ordinary occurrence, yet follows with a most dramatic
episode (Jn 5:1-18). Jesus goes to Jerusalem for the feast of
Pentecost (it could also have been Passover). An ordinary
thing for a Jew to do. In Jerusalem there is a pool, Bethesda,
where the sick and infirm gathered in order to obtain relief
(or healing) by being placed in the medicinal waters. One of
those seeking a healing was a man "who had been ill for thirty-
eight years." Again, none of this is extraordinary.

And then it happens. Jesus takes note of the sick man and
says to him, "Do you want to be well?" What an insensitive
question! Certainly Jesus must have know this man wanted to

be healed. Where is the compassion we have come to expect
from Jesus? Jesus' question seems to imply that this poor man
doesn't want to be healed. Jesus seems to be blaming the victim.

The man does not answer Jesus' question. Rather, he tries
to explain why he has been ill for so long. "Sir, I have no one
to put me into the pool... while I am on my way, someone else
gets down there before me." In other words, "it's not my fault
I have been sick all these years. I don't have help getting into
the pool. Others are too busy and my relatives are caught up
in their own lives. Besides, I am not swift enough to get into
the pool. No one waits for me." None of this answers the crucial question of Jesus: "Do you want to be well?"

Jesus knew that it takes great courage to accept healing.
Walking on one's own can be a frightening thing. There is a
certain attractiveness for the man to remain on his mat. There
is a high level of comfort which can come to those who are the
object of others' pity. If one is sick one is excused from the
responsibility of making one's way through life. Life on the mat,
the status of being sick or infirm, brings certain benefits: others provide for your needs; not much is expected of you; others are willing to overlook many of your shortcomings; and you
can always blame your condition when things don't work out.
It takes courage to reject all this and walk. Yet this is exactly
what Jesus says, "Rise, take up your mat, and walk."

Healing is not limited to the physical realm. Jesus is above
all the Divine Physician who comes to heal us of the deadly
effects of sin. Spiritual healing can require more courage than
even picking up our mat and walking. Spiritual healing must
break the chains of guilt and shame. Yet the past can work its
destructive power so that we come to despair of ever finding
a new way of living. And even if a new way is offered, sin leaves
us fearful. We are afraid of what Jesus might be asking of us.

We become uncertain and insecure about the future. The old ways, no matter how painful, look attractive because they are familiar. Who knows, in giving up one demon we might become possessed by one seven times worse. As the Irish say: "Better the devil you know than the one you don't know." The principalities and powers which keep us from responding to Jesus always play on our fears and insecurities. It is as if we hear a voice inside saying, "You will fail; you won't measure up; once a sinner always a sinner; you are only headed for more disappointment and pain."

Jesus continues to speak his liberating word, "Rise, take up your mat, and walk." The truth that sets us free requires the courage to walk with Jesus. This truth is that we *can* live a new way. We *can* be reborn in the Spirit and live as new creatures. In spite of all the voices of failure and despair the message of hope penetrates to the heart. Love drives out all fear.

There are many voices which loudly clamor to keep the women of abortion securely on their mat of guilt and shame. There are voices which offer a breezy dismissal to their pain and sense of loss. These voices within and without counsel a rejection of reconciliation. They assure us that at the end of the day there will only be more hurt and no healing. For to accept Jesus' invitation to healing requires too much. There must be a willingness to acknowledge the wrongness of abortion. There must be the strength to work through one's grief over the death of the unborn child. There must be that openness to grace which alone can heal the wound in one's heart. There must be a formal confession of the sin of abortion. There is even the call to be active in promoting greater respect for human life.

All of this is much beyond our poor capacity. Aren't we just setting up women for the very despair the Pope wanted to replace with hope?

Hail Mary!

To be sure the road back for the women of abortion is beyond their all-too-human capacity. If women were simply required to heal themselves, this would indeed be a prescription for failure. Yet such is not the case. In the words of the *Magnificat*:

> He has looked upon his servant
> in her lowliness; ...
> God who is mighty has done great
> things for me, ...
> His mercy is from age to age ...
> (He) raised the lowly ...
> Ever mindful of his mercy (Lk 1:46-55).

It may seem strange to connect Mary and her *Magnificat* with the contemporary women of abortion. Mary is the holy, pure virgin in whom the Word will take on flesh. Mary is the sinless Mother of Jesus, the Mother of God, who will be crowned as Queen of Heaven. Mary is the model of discipleship for the Church in bringing Jesus to others. Mary is the "deeply troubled" mother who says yes (*fiat*) and trusts that God's grace is sufficient. Mary goes "in haste" to be with Elizabeth. At the mere hearing of Mary's voice the child in Elizabeth's womb "leaps for joy." Mary carries the One who is Life and gives birth to the Child who is "destined for the fall and rise of many." Throughout, Mary treasures all those things in a heart that will be pierced with the sword of love.

Not in spite of but *because* of all these, Mary is the woman, mother, and disciple who speaks to the hearts of the women of abortion. Mary experiences her own unplanned pregnancy. She faces rejection and hardship from a world which has no

room for its Lord. Hence Mary is not unfamiliar with the anxi-
ety women face who find themselves pregnant in difficult circumstances. Her way of facing the challenge is to *accept, receive*
all that God sends. Mary does not turn to her own resources
and powers. These are quite limited. What is unlimited is
God's grace which makes all things possible. Mary knows she
cannot face her role in salvation history alone. She needs Jo-
seph, relatives and friends, and above all grace. Throughout,
she draws strength from knowing that in human weakness God
is at work. Even in the stable there is the presence of the holy.
In the darkness of the night there shines a star. Out of the
silence of heaven come the voices of the heavenly hosts. The
Child is not received by his own, yet the wise bring their gifts
to the One who is pure gift.

The contemporary woman of abortion, and women who
face difficult circumstances concerning a pregnancy, can turn
to Mary. She teaches that in all things we can trust completely
in God's grace. This does not mean that pain and hardship
cease. Mary's life is not a fairy tale but the story of a real woman
who believed God's word. Mary reveals that true liberation
comes to the one who submits, accepts, and receives God's
grace. Mary has the courage to say, "Let it be according to Your
will."

Mary speaks to women today:

> At this moment you may be filled with fear and ridden
> with anxiety. Pressures surround you on all sides. No
> doubt your family and friends want to support you, but
> at times you must choose what is right and not easy. This
> is one such time. Choose life. Regardless of the
> circumstances, the Lord will supply your every need. Yes
> there will be difficulties. I knew them myself. But I also
> know that being open to divine love drives out all fear.
> For through Him we can do all things because He has

given us all things. Resist the temptation to end the life within you. You may see through a glass darkly now, but there will slowly dawn that light which makes all things clear. In time you will see the wisdom of choosing life.

For those of you who have had an abortion remember God is rich in mercy. Yes, the decision for an abortion has left a wound in your heart. Yes, your decision was terribly wrong. But this is not the unforgivable sin. Heaven waits to rejoice at your reconciliation. This is no offer of cheap grace and a quick fix. The journey to healing comes at a dear price. Along the way discouragement and despair are constant companions. Also traveling with you is the Spirit who makes all things new. This is the same Spirit who will strengthen you for the victory of life.

Commencement

We have come a long way with our reflections on the magnificent words of Pope John Paul II. His special words for the women of abortion come from the heart of a Pastor who understands. There has been no attempt to deny the reality of sin. There has been every attempt to reveal the healing power of grace. Both are necessary for authentic reconciliation.

As we come to the end of our time together, the work of the Spirit has only just begun. For *The Gospel of Life*, with its special word to the women of abortion, points us toward the future with a spirit of hope and confidence. Women who have had abortions are offered a new beginning and the challenge to witness on behalf of *all* life.

The Pope takes great pains to tell women that the Church is ever ready to assist them in their return to the Lord through Reconciliation and the Eucharist. The special word by the

Pope to the women of abortion is very much related to a special word addressed to the Church in his encyclical letter *On The Mercy of God* back in 1980. In that beautiful encyclical we read:

> *The Church* lives an authentic life when she *professes and proclaims mercy* — The most stupendous attribute of the Creator and of the Redeemer — and when she brings people close to the sources of the Savior's Mercy, of which she is the trustee and dispenser. ...the Church professes and proclaims conversion. Conversion to God always consists in *discovering His Mercy,* that is, in discovering that love which is patient and kind as only the Creator and Father can be ... Conversion to God is always the first of the "rediscovery" of this Father, who is rich in mercy (No. 13).

The Father of Mercy, through his Church entrusted with the message of mercy, reaches out to the women of abortion.

> Do not lose hope but let the wound in your heart be healed.
> Let your healing be a source of strength for others.
> May you live each day as an eloquent defender of all human life and help others to respect life in all its forms. In so doing, you will help build the civilization of life and love.

Resources

The following is a brief list of reading material that will prove valuable in supplementing the reflections contained in this book.

Barnard, C., *The Long Term Psychosocial Effects of Abortion* (1990).

Burke, T.K., PhD, *Rachel's Vineyard* (Alba House, 1995).

Doka, K., *Disenfranchised Grief* (Jossey-Bass, 1989).

Mannion, Michael, *Post-Abortion Aftermath* (Sheed & Ward, 1994).

_____, *Abortion and Healing: A Cry to be Whole* (Sheed & Ward, 1986).

_____, *Psycho-Spiritual Healing After Abortion* (with Douglas Crawford; Sheed & Ward, 1989).

McDonnell, K., *Not An Easy Choice* (LPC InBook, 1984).

McGrath, E., *Women & Depression: Risk Factors and Treatment Issues* (American Psychological Assn., 1990).

McGuire, Kristen, *The Glory to Be Revealed in You* (Alba House, 1995).

Selby, T., *The Mourning After: Help for Post-Abortion Syndrome* (Baker Bks., 1990).

Shostak, A., *Men and Abortion: Lessons, Losses & Love* (Praeger Pubs., 1984).

Vaughan, H., *Canonical Variates of Post-Abortion Syndrome* (1991).

In addition to the above reading materials a good deal of support can be provided by **Project Rachael** and **Women**

of Jericho. Further information on these organizations can be obtained from one's parish or diocesan pro-life office.

In addition, parishes and respect life ministries can provide a significant amount of spiritual counseling.

The local diocese can provide guidance in finding a priest for spiritual counseling. Naturally, if it is prudent, one's pastor is an obvious person to turn to for spiritual guidance and sacramental healing.